THE
WORLD
outside
Our Door

THE
WORLD
outside
Our Door

Elizabeth Hawkins

ARCHWAY
PUBLISHING

Archway Publishing books may be ordered through booksellers or by contacting:

Archway Publishing
1663 Liberty Drive
Bloomington, IN 47403
www.archwaypublishing.com
1 (888) 242-5904

ISBN: 978-1-4808-4889-4 (sc)
ISBN: 978-1-4808-4890-0 (e)

Library of Congress Control Number: 2017909676

Print information available on the last page.

Archway Publishing rev. date: 06/13/2020

This book is dedicated to the memory of my brother John Frederick Smith, Jr., who passed away on June 11, 2017.

Acknowledgments

I first want to thank my mother, Elsie Smith, for encouraging and supporting me my entire life. I want to thank my brothers, Rodney and John, for providing me with their perspective of our father. Finally, I want to thank Natasha Small, the best writing coach ever, for sticking with me through this incredible journey.

Chapter 1

OXON HILL, MARYLAND

March 24, 1983

The gold Cadillac hearse pulled up in front of the Southview Garden apartment complex, which Liz and her mother, Elsie, shared with her father, Fred. The driver from Pope's Funeral Home arrived at the appointed time to escort the Smith family to the chapel, where Fred's wake had been held the night before.

Liz gazed out the patio door, which faced the parking lot. She stood in the very spot where she and her mother had found Fred standing, one bitterly cold February night, with tears in his eyes. They'd returned home from an evening church service. The patio door had been cracked open, and there had stood Fred, gasping for air. Liz's father had been in the final stage of emphysema, and his inability to breathe frightened him. He had felt alone and abandoned. Terror filled his eyes. He had known he was dying. He hadn't wanted to die alone.

Liz immediately called an ambulance, and Fred was transported to nearby Greater Southeast Community Hospital. It would be the first of many calls and hospital stays for Fred over the next two years.

"The limo is here," Liz, still peering out the patio door, called to her family.

How tacky, she thought as she looked at the stark, gold vehicle. *Are they kidding?*

Liz preferred the traditional, black hearse or even a white one, but this gold monstrosity was just hideous.

Fred would not be happy with this, she thought.

She found it easier to fixate on the gold funeral car than on her feelings of incredible sadness. Nothing in her life had been more painful than Fred's death. Yet she could not let the incredibly sad occasion and her grief engulf her. Liz would be strong.

The funeral was held on Thursday at noon. Although it was officially springtime, the temperature registered a cold thirty-six degrees.

The last five days since her father's passing had seemed to move in slow motion for Liz. She had felt frozen in time. Now standing at the patio door about to travel in the unsightly gold hearse, she still was not quite able to snap out of her trance.

The family—her eldest brother, Rodney, and his wife, Joanette; Liz's brother John and his five-year-old daughter, Yavonne; and Aunt Bernice, Elsie's eldest sister from Indianapolis—had congregated in the living room. Liz gathered her belongings and held open the door as the family filed out, one by one, to get into the limousine.

Before leaving, Liz glanced back into the apartment and scanned the perimeter of the room. Her eyes focused on the apricot swivel chair where her father had always sat. In that moment, it dawned on her that she would never see him sitting there again.

* * *

The ride to the funeral home was quiet. Liz peered out the window the entire time. Her father was dead, and the memories of the past twenty-one years of her life with him slide projected in her mind, one scene after another.

Practicality was the hallmark of this clan. Even the way Liz's mother had informed one of her sisters about Fred's passing would have caused Fred to chuckle. Elsie had tried for two days to contact her sister Willie Bea in Pensacola, Florida, to let her know about Fred. Willie Bea's phone had stayed busy.

"This gal has got her phone off the hook again," Elsie had said to a newly-arrived Bernice, mad as hell. "Always afraid somebody is gonna get in her damn business."

Bernice had suggested she send Willie Bea a telegram. At Western Union, Elsie, who had still been displeased about all the trouble she had to go through to contact Willie Bea, had written a curt message that read, "Fred's dead." Bernice had balked at the wording and changed it to read, "Freddie died."

When they returned and told Liz the story, Liz cracked up laughing. That was her mother—straightforward and to the point.

Liz smiled and thought, *Fred would have laughed his head off about all this.*

Fred had always been Liz's protector, especially when it had come to her brothers. She remembered the time Fred had to hold back an outraged John, her second-oldest brother, after Liz had stepped on his and Rodney's model cars. They had worked hard gluing the pieces together and painting and decaling them. But the cars had been destroyed in one fell swoop when little Liz stepped on them, deciding that they were roller skates. Fred, who had just come home from work and still been in his military uniform, had to lift Liz over his head—her back parallel with the ceiling—to prevent John from pummeling her like a piñata.

"Now, now, brother. She's just a baby," Fred had often told the boys after one of Liz's mischievous acts.

"I don't want to hear that baby stuff!" John had shouted. "You always say that."

Fred had often recounted this and other stories about Liz and her brothers' childhood to her, especially when he had been drinking. As she had grown older, his drinking would be a source of embarrassment for her and his retelling of these stories would be annoying. But now her father was gone. His drunken stories seemed more precious now than unnerving.

After a fifteen-minute drive, the limousine arrived at the funeral home. Liz led the way as the family entered the chapel in lockstep where Fred lay.

The night before, Liz had been in detached mode. She had refused to ride to the wake in the limousine with the family, insisting on driving herself in her father's 1976 pea-green Chevrolet Caprice. The limousine ride would have made her father's death too real. She couldn't handle that yet. She had also refused to help plan funeral arrangements. Liz hated discomfort. Planning her father's funeral definitely qualified as heartrending discomfort, so she had decided to avoid as much of the inevitable as possible.

As a little girl, Liz often hidden in the closet, under the kitchen sink, or under her bedcover in an attempt to escape from the rest of the world when she had felt anxious. She had pretended that the world outside her door—the world too gritty and harsh—hadn't existed. That way, she had been able to detach herself from any unpleasant situation, if only in her own head. Thankfully, Rodney and John had stepped up and helped Elsie with the funeral arrangements.

At the wake, Liz had dreaded seeing her father in a casket. She had only looked from a distance. She had allowed herself to be distracted by entertaining the many friends and family members in attendance. But today would be her last chance to see him, so she mustered up her courage and entered the chapel to see her father one last time.

Liz stood in front of the casket and looked down at her father. Sleeping—he looked as though he was sleeping. Liz raised her hand to touch him but decided against it. She felt like she wanted to cry, but no tears came.

You were a good daughter, she thought. *There is no need for tears or guilt. You did right by your father.*

She had attended many funerals in the past and had often heard her mother say that guilt was behind all that whooping and hollering people did at funerals.

Aunt Bernice stepped up and stood beside her.

"He looks at peace," she whispered, interrupting Liz's thoughts.

Liz did not reply. She had a tight grip on the side of the casket. Her muscles tensed as if she was trying to prevent herself from falling over. She held her gaze on Fred's face.

She recalled him sleeping after working the midnight shift while she had quietly played with her dolls in her parents' room. She decided that this would be how she would remember him—not dead in a casket but sleeping in bed after working the midnight shift.

Liz looked into Aunt Bernice's tear-filled eyes, sucked in her breath, and bit her bottom lip. Standing so close to her aunt, Liz again felt like crying, but she refused to let a tear drop or to whoop and holler like the guilt-ridden mourners her mother had told her about. Crying meant making a spectacle of yourself, and Liz would not embarrass herself. She had to stay strong. She patted Bernice on the back, turned on her heels, and then took a seat on the front pew.

After a few minutes, more guests arrived. Liz's best friend, Tina, came over with her boyfriend. Liz stood and embraced Tina. She could feel herself fold into Tina's arms. This person who had been like a sister to her for the past sixteen years was here to support her, and she appreciated it.

Liz stood back and looked at her friend. "Thanks for coming."

"Sure," said Tina. "You know I'm here for you, sis. But I hope you don't mind if we don't go to the cemetery. I just don't do cemeteries."

"It's okay," Liz replied. She wished she did not have to go to the cemetery either.

"Thanks," Tina said, looking relieved.

The service began with Reverend King, the funeral-home minister, officiating. Liz had never known her father to attend church. In fact, he had not attended church since he had been a child in Southport, North Carolina, when he had occasionally attended services at St. James Methodist church under the Reverend Samuel Frink.

As the organist played an instrumental hymn, Liz fixated on the program that she had typed and copied at school. It was her only contribution to her father's service. She was enrolled at Strayer College in pursuit of her associate degree.

He's not going to see me graduate from college, she thought.

"I will be reading from the twenty-third psalm," Reverend King said, bringing Liz out of her meditative state. "The Lord is my shepherd; I shall not want," he read.

Liz recalled that this had been her father's favorite scripture in the Bible. He had been able to recite it by heart. She remembered her father helping her memorize scriptures that her Bible-school teacher had assigned to her. He had been proud when she had learned her verses and recited them effortlessly. His pride in her had pleased her. But her feelings for her father were ambivalent—a mixture of both the positive and the negative. Liz tended to focus on the positive and to block out the negative.

Liz's mental slide projector turned on again and blocked out the funeral service. She remembered sitting in a dark stairwell. It had been the day her father had forgotten to pick her up from kindergarten in 1967. Fred had retired from the air force the year before and had been tasked with getting Liz to and from school each day. As usual, he had been drinking and had fallen asleep. Needless to say, he had overslept and had been late picking Liz up.

On this particular day, Liz had taken the initiative to walk home by herself. Besides, no kid likes to be the last one to get picked up from school. It had been easy to get home because there had been a crossing guard at every street.

When Liz arrived at their four-unit apartment building on Portland Street in southeast Washington, she knocked on the door and stood proud and ready to tell her father she had come home all by herself. But no one answered the door. She had seen her father's brown Chevy parked in front of the building, so she had been sure he was inside.

Unfazed, she sat on the fourth step of the stairwell and had begun to read the book she had borrowed from the bookmobile that day, entitled, *Sam, Bangs, and Moonshine*. She had only picked the book because it had a cat on the cover. In later years, cats would prove to be her favorite pet.

All of a sudden, Liz saw her father bolt from the apartment, not even noticing her on the steps. When he had returned after about twenty minutes, he had been surprised to see her sitting in the stairwell looking unconcerned.

"How long have you been sitting there?" Fred had asked his daughter.

She hunched her shoulders up and down.

"I don't know," Liz had responded in a nonchalant manner.

"Well, did you see me when I came out?" Fred asked.

"Yes."

"Well, why didn't you say something?"

"I didn't know where you were going," Liz had replied most sincerely.

Fred released a heavy sigh of exasperation. On the one hand, he had been annoyed with Liz for not calling out to him when she had seen him rush out the door. He had been out of his mind with worry when he hadn't been able to find her at the school.

Driving home, a strong sense of dread had overwhelmed him at the thought of having to call his wife to explain that he had lost their daughter. He had been relieved to find her there safe, sound, and seemingly unscathed over the event, but he had still been a little ticked that she hadn't stopped him before he had rushed out.

"Well, come on inside," Fred said. "Let's get you something to eat."

* * *

"This concludes this part of the funeral service for Mr. John Frederick Smith," Reverend King announced.

His sermon was short and sweet, just as Liz liked sermons to be. She had grown up attending a number of Pentecostal, Apostolic, and Holy Roller types of churches where the preachers' sermons went on into the night.

I swear, some of those ministers could preach the hell out of you, then preach the hell right back into you, being so long-winded, she thought.

"The interment will take place at Arlington National Cemetery," he continued.

The organist played a soft hymn, "Nearer, My God, to Thee," and those in attendance followed behind the white casket as it exited the building to be transported to its final destination.

At Arlington Cemetery, Fred was given a military burial. During the traditional playing of "Taps" by the bugler in the key of B-flat, Liz recited the first stanza in her mind.

Day is done, gone the sun,

From the lake, from the hill, from the sky.

All is well, safely rest,

God is nigh.

Standing at the grave site and shivering from the cold, Liz recalled her brothers, John and Rodney's claim that they had seen something floating up toward the sky on the night Fred had died. They had both been on the patio taking a smoke when it had occurred. They surmised it had been a phenomenon—Fred's spirit ascending to the heavens. Liz wished that she had witnessed the miraculous event.

The first shot of the twenty-one-gun salute startled Liz. She was scheduled to report to basic training at Fort Jackson in Columbia, South Carolina, the following month in April. The previous month, Fred had gotten to see Liz in her army fatigues. She had already been attending weekend drills with her army reserve unit at Fort Belvoir in Virginia. The last one had been held on the weekend of her twenty-first birthday. She had told her father that she would be going to basic training in April.

"How do you like my uniform?" Liz had asked while standing in the doorway of her father's bedroom.

"Nice," Fred said with a slight nod as he sat on the side of his bed.

"I'll be going to Fort Jackson next month for basic training. I hope I make it," Liz had said while feeling trepidation.

"I think you'll make it," her father had assured in a voice just above a whisper.

He would never know that she hadn't made it through basic training. She had failed to complete the required amount of push-ups for the physical fitness test. Rather than restart the eight-week training from the beginning, Liz had opted for an uncharacterized discharge. The army discharge had not been honorable or dishonorable. It had been like she was never there.

The training had been hard, and Liz had found the change from a civilian lifestyle to a military one to be uncomfortable. It had been easier for her to walk away from the military and return to a life she had been familiar with, rather than see it through or put forth a real effort to successfully complete basic training. She had returned home and completed her associate degree program at Strayer College, but her actions had sent her on a trajectory of taking the easier paths in life rather than challenging ones.

The wind chill in the open area of the cemetery was unforgiving.

Liz looked down at her five-year-old niece, Yavonne, who was wearing a navy-blue spring coat with red trim. The coat provided little protection from the cold and someone had put their oversized gloves on Yavonne's hands in a well-meaning but unproductive measure to stave off the elements.

At the time of his death, Fred had three granddaughters— Yavonne, Yavonne's nine-year-old half-sister, Kenji, who lived in Georgia, and Rodney's daughter, ten-month-old Regina. Yavonne had been the one Fred knew best, and she had been his heart. He had loved that she called him Papa. She had become a faithful, little helper during his last days. If he had wanted something, he would ring a handheld, brass bell.

When Yavonne had heard the bell, she had run to his side to inquire, "Did you ring the bell Papa?" Yavonne had been so excited to help.

"Yes. Will you bring me a piece of ice?" He had once requested from Yavonne.

She had returned with only one ice cube, had handed it to him, and had returned to playing with her doll. When Liz entered the room, her father had asked her to bring him a glass and had nearly lost his breath laughing at his granddaughter's innocence.

Liz had brought Fred the glass grudgingly, because she had known he would drop his ice cube in it and dig out a pint of liquor he had had stashed behind his favorite apricot swivel chair. His drinking had always been a source of resentment for her. She loved her father but had seen his drinking as a weakness. And it had made her mad as hell.

* * *

When the military chaplain announced that the service had concluded, Liz and her family made a beeline to the gold limousine for the return ride home. As it pulled away, Liz felt overcome with anxiety as she watched her father's still aboveground casket disappear in the distance. Her chest felt as if it were tightening. She could hardly breathe.

He's all alone now, she thought, and that made her sad.

Her mind took her back to the 1965 funeral of Fred's mother, Dora. Although she had only been three years old, Liz recalled feeling a sense of panic when she had seen the casket of her grandmother being lowered into the ground. In an instant, Liz had attempted to leap onto the casket as it descended. A quick reacting Fred grabbed little Liz by the back of the coat and had kept her from plummeting into the open grave.

What was I thinking? Liz now wondered.

She had recalled reading her Grandma Dora's obituary when she had put the program together for her father's service. She had been astonished to see that Fred's mother, Dora, had died on March 19, 1965, at 7:00 p.m., while Fred had died on March 19, 1983, at 8:30 p.m., eighteen years later.

Liz's mother told her that before Fred died she had heard him whisper, "I'm coming Momma."

This was another phenomenon that Liz had not witnessed. She thought she had been as close to her father as anyone else in the family—even closer. She wondered why she had not heard his final words or witnessed his *spiritual ascent.*

When the limousine finally arrived back at the apartment, Liz led the way inside. She headed straight for her room and closed the door behind her. On her twin-sized bed, she curled herself into a fetal position, placed the pillow over her head, and cried for the next hour and a half.

Gone was the man who had treated her as though she had hung the stars and the moon, who had believed that she could be the best that she could be, and for whom he had been most proud. But Liz had not always proud of her father.

She hated his drinking. She thought that he hid behind it and had used it as a crutch to hide his faults and insecurities. She hated his smoking too, which had ultimately taken his life. He had been just five months shy of his seventieth birthday. Now he was gone, and in the twenty-one years that she had with him, Liz could not remember when he had not been drinking. For the rest of her life, she would cherish the good memories and blot out the shame and resentment her father's drinking had caused.

Liz finally cried herself to sleep. She dreamed of her father's ascension toward the heavens and entrance into a better place.

Chapter 2

PENSACOLA, FLORIDA

Early 1950's

Elsie sat wide-legged on the back porch with a bucket of soiled diapers at her feet. It was the crack of dawn on Saturday, and the breeze from the Gulf of Mexico was a cool relief for what promised to be another hot July day in Pensacola. She crinkled her nose at the smell of urine and feces, which emanated from the bucket.

Sweating, Elsie plunged one diaper at a time into the tub of hot water. Using lye soap, she worked up suds and scrubbed the stained cotton squares against the metal ripples of the washboard. One by one, she squeezed out the excess water in each diaper. Then she hung all of them on a line stretched between two porch beams, which were attached to the rented two-bedroom house she shared with three housemates.

As the sun shone over the horizon, Elsie drifted into a light trance. Rubbing the diapers up and down the washboard in methodical motions lulled the young woman into an imaginary world of romance minus chores. Elsie desired a beau and dreamed that someday her prince would come. Apparently, his car had broken down, or no one had bothered to tell him that Elsie awaited his entrance, for there was no sign of the prince anywhere.

A rude thump at the back fence jolted Elsie from her quasi daydream. The sturdiness of the porch slats felt extra hard against her bottom as she looked toward the sound. Because her vision was obscured by a low-hanging willow tree, Elsie narrowed her eyes as a tall, slim man emerged through the thicket. Her expression softened for a moment.

Who is this good-looking guy cutting through my yard? She wondered.

She was wary of the stranger, however, and she quickly regained a curt expression.

"Good morning ma'am," the stranger said with a broad smile. He took in a deep breath, "Your baby's diapers certainly do smell sweet."

Listen to this garbage, Elsie thought. *Who ever heard of diapers smelling sweet?*

"What are you doing in my yard?" Elsie wanted to know.

"Oh, I was just taking a shortcut," he replied still smiling.

Elsie couldn't help but notice how handsome the stranger was. He wore civilian clothes with polished military shoes. She assumed he was in the navy since Fort Barrancas was in Pensacola. He looked to be nearly six feet tall, stood straight as an arrow, and had a nice pecan-brown complexion, dreamy eyes, and long eyelashes.

"Well, next time go around the long way. Now get on out of my yard, you little fresh-ass sailor," she scolded.

The handsome stranger nodded in a gentlemanly manner of acceptance and exited the yard.

"What's going on?" her roommate Katie asked after hearing voices in the backyard.

"It's nothing, girl. It was just some navy guy taking a shortcut through the yard."

"Well if he had any food with him, you jumped the gun on shooing him away so fast."

Both women chuckled.

"Seriously," Katie continued, "We're getting low on food. Do you think you'll be able to get something from your father's icebox?"

"Sure, no problem," Elsie said checking her watch. "In fact I'd better get over there now. Daddy and Cornelius should be leaving for work any minute."

"Okay. Hey, thanks for washing my baby's diapers. You didn't have to do that."

"I know. I was just up early and decided to do them before it got too hot."

With that, Elsie jumped off the porch and ran the five blocks to her father's house on West LaRua Street. Stealing food from her father's refrigerator was Elsie's way of helping her housemates out.

At twenty-one years of age, Elsie had felt that it was long overdue for her to strike out on her own. All her friends were already married with children and starting to call her a spinster and an old maid.

Her first line of business had been to move out of her fathers' house. So she moved into a quaint two-bedroom house with twenty-six-year-old Katie, who had two small children by two different fathers and no prospects of marriage. The pair had later been joined by Lily, a forty-year-old, married woman, who had separated from her husband, and Helen, a twenty-eight-year-old barmaid.

Both Katie and Lily worked as housekeepers. Since Elsie didn't work, she did the majority of the household chores, cooking and babysitting Katie's children when she was at work. The three other women split the fifteen-dollars-a-month rent, the monthly utility bill, and food costs. However, by the end of the month, they always seemed to run short on food.

Elsie hid behind the sycamore tree near her father's house

and waited until she saw him get into the car with his coworker, who gave him a lift to work. A few minutes later, she saw her stepmother leave the house for her job too. When she thought the coast was clear, Elsie snuck around to the rear of the house and entered through the back door with her set of keys. However, her cat-burglar tactics fooled no one.

"When you buy groceries this week, make sure you get extra for Elsie," her father, Sam, had instructed his wife when she had been leaving for the grocery store. "She'll be sneaking in here, around the end of the month, raiding the refrigerator."

* * *

Katie returned home after working all day. She was tired. The first thing she did was kick off her shoes and then check on her babies who were asleep in the bedroom they all shared. She entered the kitchen where Elsie was cooking. Elsie looked up when she saw Katie.

"I got some steaks," Elsie said with a twinge of excitement.

"I see. They smell good. Can't wait to eat."

Katie stepped out onto the back porch to take a smoke. After taking a few drags, she was surprised by a sudden thump and then by a figure emerging through the tree branches.

"Shit! You scared me," Katie gulped out while holding her chest.

"Sorry ma'am. I was wondering if the lady that was washing her baby's diapers this morning is here."

Katie raised her eyebrow and stared at the handsome stranger who held a handful of yellow daffodils, which he had obviously just pulled from somebody's yard.

"I'm the only one here that has a baby," she answered.

"Oh, I met another lady right out here this morning washing diapers. I wondered if I could see her again."

"Elsie," Katie called out while turning her head slightly over her left shoulder but never taking her eyes off the handsome stranger.

"Yeah," Elsie called back.

"There is someone out here to see you. Said he met you this morning when you were washing *your* baby's diapers."

Elsie took the food off the stove and came out the back door wiping her hands on her apron.

"You again," she exclaimed. "Didn't I tell you not to cut through my yard?"

"Yes, you did, and I'm sorry about that."

"You should be sorry," Katie interrupted. "You damn near gave me a heart attack."

Katie chuckled, extinguished her cigarette, and went back into the house.

"So, your friend called you Elsie."

"Yes, I'm Elsie."

"Elsie what?"

"Elsie Underwood. What's with the third degree, and why are you back here?"

"I'm Fred Smith. I wanted to see you again and give you these." Fred held out the flowers to Elsie.

"Whose yard did you steal these flowers from? It better not have been one of my neighbors," Elsie said, taking the flowers. She eyed Fred up and down.

"No, nothing like that. I just really wanted to talk to you and wondered if you'd like to catch a movie or something sometime. I'm here in Pensacola just about every weekend."

"Where are you the other days?

"Fort Walton Air Force Base."

"Air force. I thought you were navy."

"I know. You called me a fresh sailor. That tickled me."

"Yeah, well I can't make any promises, but you can come around next weekend if you want. Just don't be hopping my back fence."

Fred threw back his head and laughed, exposing his front gold tooth and top gold fillings.

"All right. It's a deal," Fred said as he exited the yard through the front gate.

Elsie watched him as he walk away. He had a spry gait and walked with his head held high like he had every confidence in the world that he could get anything he wanted, including her.

Well it's not going to be that easy Mr. Fred Smith, Elsie thought as she returned to the kitchen, tossing the stolen daffodils in the trash can.

* * *

"Hello ma'am, remember me? I was here last weekend."

"Yes. Fred, right?"

"That's right."

Katie looked Fred up and down while taking a drag off her cigarette. She looked toward the sky and released rings of smoke.

"I'm Katie, by the way," she finally said. "Elsie ain't here right now but she said if I seen you today to ask if you'd clean up the yard for her."

"Sure, I'd be glad to," Fred responded.

"Okay then. Well the rake is in the shed out back," Katie said as she rose to enter the house.

After doing Elsie's yard work, Fred stuck around the house for hours entertaining the other ladies. Katie, Helen, and Lily all found Fred to be quite charming, and he made them laugh. Elsie did not come home until long after Fred had left.

"Girl, I can't believe that man cleaned the yard for you," Helen exclaimed.

"Yeah, he seems to be smitten with you. No telling what else you can get him to do," Lily chimed in.

"Chil' that man is tryin' get that kitty cat," Katie said laughing.

"Girl, you oughta know," Lily joked.

Elsie smiled as her roommates teased her.

"I think I will test Lily's theory," Elsie finally said.

"What do you mean?" Katie asked.

"Next time he comes by, one of y'all tell him to clean the kitchen for me."

They all roared with laughter.

For the next six weeks, Elsie referred to Fred as her "puppet on a string." She was never home when Fred came to call, but she left him a chore list, and he completed every task for her, including cleaning the bathroom, mopping the floors, and picking up a block of ice for the icebox. When he took her punishment for a month and a half, Elsie decided to be home the next time he came by.

"Finally," Fred exclaimed when it was Elsie who answered the door. "I was expecting one of the ladies to give me your latest instructions," Fred said.

Elsie laughed.

"No, I'm home today," she said motioning for him to come in.

They sat on the sofa and talked for what seemed like hours. She learned that he was from Southport, North Carolina, had moved to Norfolk, Virginia, when he was a teenager, and had first joined the army but then re-enlisted in the air force.

"So, do you like being in the military?"

"Well, it's a roof over my head, money in my pocket, free medical care, and three squares a day, so I can't complain. Speaking of three squares, I'm getting a little wolfie."

Elsie shot Fred a curious look.

"Wolfie?" What's that mean?

"I just mean I'm getting hungry. You know, hungry as a dog or a wolf. What you ladies got to eat around here?"

"I don't know. You can check the icebox."

Fred got up and went to the kitchen. He looked in the refrigerator and frowned. There was a pack of baloney with only two slices left.

"Y'all need some groceries in here," Fred yelled, still leaning into the refrigerator.

"So, take me to Del Shanks Grocers."

"Del Shanks? They're kinda high. What about Piggly Wiggly?"

"No. I don't buy from Piggly Wiggly. The meat at Del Shanks is much fresher."

"Fine," Fred conceded. "I'll buy. You cook."

"That's a deal," Elsie beamed.

* * *

"Here you are, Sergeant Smith," Mr. Goodman said handing Fred the keys to a two-bedroom, cozy bungalow, which sat in the middle of a cul-de-sac. After six months of dating, Fred and Elsie were expecting their first child and were moving in together. Mr. Goodman was happy to rent to a military couple because it ensured a steady payment.

"Thanks, Mr. Goodman," Fred replied.

"I hope you and your growing family will be very happy here."

"I'm sure we will," Fred said, closing the door as Mr. Goodman stepped off the front porch. Elsie was already looking around the tiny dwelling and determining where all the furniture would be placed.

When their son Rodney was born in September 1953, all the neighbors in the cul-de-sac and Elsie's three former roommates, Katie, Lily, and Helen came to see her new bundle of joy.

"Aw, he is a fine-looking baby," Katie commented, looking down into the wooden cradle in the living room where the sleeping infant lay.

"Yep, and he looks just like his daddy," Helen chimed in.

A hard knock on the front door startled Helen. She jumped.

"Ooh, who could this be?" she said while opening the front door.

"Hello," Mr. Goodman and his wife said in unison.

"We come with gifts for you and your baby boy," said Mrs. Goodman, entering the house behind her husband. Mr. Goodman held a large fruit basket.

Trying to contain her excitement, Elsie's eyes widened. "My goodness, Mr. Goodman, what do you have there?"

"I know how much you and Fred love fruit," he replied.

"This is for the baby," Mrs. Goodman said to Elsie while handing her a large paper bag.

Elsie opened the bag with great anticipation. She pulled out a box and opened it. It was a beautiful silver-plated comb and brush set. Also in the bag was a porcelain piggy bank filled with coins.

"Oh boy, a piggy bank ... and there's money already in it," Elsie exclaimed, shaking the bank gently.

"Yes," Mr. Goodman said proudly, "there's five dollars' worth of quarters in that bank."

"Wow! That's big money. Fred and I can't thank you enough." Elsie didn't hide her tears.

When Fred returned home from work, Elsie couldn't wait to show him the gifts from the Goodmans.

"Look Fred, the Goodmans brought over this big basket of fruit for us."

"That's nice," Fred said as he took a seat on the sofa.

"And that's not all. They brought this beautiful silver comb and brush set for the baby."

Fred looked at the gift but didn't show as much excitement as Elsie had. Then Elsie reached for the piggy bank, which sat on the cocktail table in front of the sofa. She shook the bank.

"Now here's the grand prize," she said beaming. "A bank filled with five dollars' worth of quarters," she exclaimed.

Reaching for the bank, Fred's eyes bucked.

"Wow! That's big money," he said with the most enthusiasm he had conveyed since he had walked through the door. Fred got up and took the bank into the nursery where his sleeping son lay in his crib.

"Look here, baby boy Smith. Your first bank," Fred whispered, placing the bank on the dresser.

He placed his hands on the side rails of the crib and gazed at Baby Rodney. At forty years old, Fred had sired his first male heir. Although his heart was filled with pride and joy, his stomach twisted with knots at the stigma his son might face being born out of wedlock. Fred knew this stigma well. It's what he had faced back in Southport.

"History will not repeat itself," Fred whispered, tugging gently on Rodney's tiny foot. "You are good enough, my boy. Good enough to bear your father's last name."

Fred would not subject Rodney to the web of lies that had been spun about this father's lineage. Fred had been a teenager when he had learned that a neighbor was really his biological father.

Fred loved his little family and worked to make everything legitimate. He consulted with the military legal staff about ensuring his son's legitimacy by signing legal documents affirming that the child was his and would bear the name Smith at birth. He also wanted to make an honest woman of Elsie and marry her, but he had a dilemma. He was already married. His wife had been committed to an asylum in Virginia over a decade ago.

Divorcing someone with a diminished mental capacity was next to impossible. But in seven shorts months, Pensacola attorneys Holdsberry and Newberry would help Fred find a legal loophole that would grant him a bill of divorce.

By February 1954, Elsie was pregnant for the second time, and by April of that year, Fred's divorce was finalized. On April 20, 1954, Fred and Elsie were married in a simple ceremony at the local courthouse. Elsie's sister Willie Bea and seven-month-old Rodney were in attendance. The following month, Fred was sent overseas to do an eighteen-month tour in Okinawa, Japan.

* * *

"How about Naoki if it's a boy?" Fred wrote in a letter to Elsie from Japan. "It means *honest tree*. If you don't like that, what about Satoru? It means *enlightened*."

"Why does he keep sending me all these Japanese names?" Elsie scoffed holding the letter up for her sister Willie Bea to read.

Her sister glanced at the letter and giggled. "I don't know chil', but what I want to know is what makes a tree honest anyway," she joked.

"Chil' please," Elsie said shaking her head. "I'm just going to write him back and tell him that if it's a boy, I'm naming him John Frederick Smith Junior. I know he doesn't want a junior, but I've made up my mind."

Elsie felt somber after making the statement. She felt that if for some reason Fred didn't make it back alive, she wanted the baby to be Fred's namesake.

"Why don't Fred want a junior anyway?" Willie Bea asked, interrupting Elsie's thoughts.

"He doesn't like the fact that John Smith is such a common name. He doesn't like it for himself. That's why he prefers to go by his middle name. I don't care though. I want the baby to be a junior if it's a boy."

On November 10, 1954, at 11:26 p.m., Elsie gave birth to John Frederick Smith Junior at the naval hospital in Pensacola. The following morning was Veterans Day, and Elsie woke to the sound of the drums and horns playing in the Veteran's Day parade on base.

When Fred returned to Pensacola in November 1955, his life with Elsie and the boys would move them away from Pensacola and begin anew when he was stationed at Bolling Air Force Base in Washington, DC.

Chapter 3

WASHINGTON, DC

December 1961

"When the moon hits your eye like a big pizza pie, that's amore." Dean Martin's record played on the turntable for the fifth time in a row. The arm on Fred's record player was up, which allowed the seven-inch, vinyl disc to play over and over again until it was manually stopped. Fred was drunk as hell.

"Sing," Fred implored eight-year-old Rodney and seven-year-old John.

Both boys stood before their father. They held the spoons Fred had demanded they hold, which served as make-believe microphones. The boys stood stoically and scarcely mouthed the words to the song.

"When the world seems to shine, like you've had too much wine, that's amore," Fred belted out along with the record.

He sat on the edge of the sofa. His eyes were closed, and he swayed side to side. Mimicking a conductor, his arms carved the air, and his hand opened and closed as if to pull taffy. Occasionally, an index finger would shoot out.

"Bells will ring, ting-a-ling-a-ling, ting-a-ling-a-ling," Fred continued with a goofy grin plastered on his face. "C'mon y'all, sing," he continued to prod his young sons.

Fred loved music and often tried to get Rodney and John to perform the songs of some of his favorite crooners like Dean Martin, Frank Sinatra, and Bing Crosby. Rodney and John resented these moments with Fred. He never interacted with the boys until he had had a few. For the most part, Fred was aloof and perhaps even indifferent when it came to his sons.

Elsie, who was seven months pregnant, finally waddled from the bedroom to rescue the boys from their father's torture.

"Listen, if I hear "That's Amore" one more time, Fred, I'm going to scream," Elsie said. She scowled at Fred. "It's late. Let them get ready for bed now."

Elsie took the spoons from the boys' hands. Rodney and John breathed a sigh of relief, happy to be done with the impromptu performance.

"Okay," Fred said yielding to his wife's wishes. "Good night, boys."

He held his arms open to hug them. This show of affection only happened when Fred was drunk.

"Good night," they said, almost in unison.

When Rodney leaned in to hug his father, he was repelled by the bitter stench of liquor and tobacco on Fred's breath combined with the fishy smell of sardines he'd eaten earlier. Rodney's hug lasted only seconds, and he quickly exited his father's presence.

When John leaned in for a hug, Fred's unshaven facial stubble scratched his cheek. It felt like a prickly-pear cactus. John stiffened. He hated that feeling. He released his hug, instinctively placed his hand to his cheek, and then turned and scurried off to his room.

John's feelings for Fred were a bit of a contradiction. He looked up to Fred. He liked the way his father looked in his uniform. He liked the way Fred stood too—back straight, chest out, and head held high. However, his admiration for his father came in brief spurts. After a few drinks, Fred morphed into someone that John abhorred.

February 11, 1962

Elsie's labor pains began on a frigid Sunday night. The temperature had dipped down into the low twenties, and the forecast called for snow later in the week. As she finished packing her bag in preparation for her hospital stay, Fred was outside warming up the old white Chevy Impala.

"Elsie, is it time for our brother to be born?" John asked.

Elsie and Fred fancied themselves as new aged, progressive parents and as such, decided that it was hip to allow their kids to call them by their first names. Besides, back when her boys were babies, Elsie had been so skinny and youthful looking, few people had believed that she was even old enough to have children.

"Yes, it's time," Elsie replied.

She ran her hand over her belly. The contractions were picking up the pace.

"You okay, Elsie?" John asked, noticing the obvious look of pain on his mother's face.

"I'm fine," she reassured her son. "But go get your coat on and go outside and let Fred know that it's time to go now."

John grabbed his coat and ran out the front door with excitement building in his little body. Elsie quickly gathered the rest of her things, and then she and Rodney followed John to the car for the twenty-minute drive to the hospital on Andrews Air Force Base. They arrived just after seven in the evening. Once Elsie was checked in, Fred and the boys returned home.

* * *

"She ain't ready yet," one nurse called out to another. After checking Elsie's cervix, she had determined that her dilation was only at three centimeters. "You just lay back and relax for a while until your cervix widens up some more," she said to Elsie who was lying on a gurney in a holding area. "We'll be right across the hall in the break room," she continued.

Elsie's pain increased over the next three hours. She could hear the two nurses talking across the hall about their husbands and children, about which doctor was the best to work with, and about which head nurse was the worst.

"Do you want cheese crackers or peanut butter crackers?" She heard one nurse ask the other.

As a distraction, when her labor pains increased, Elsie focused on whatever the two hens cackled about. When the pain subsided, she found that she could squeeze in a few minutes of sleep.

By 10:30 p.m., she was in full labor, and at 11:12 p.m., she had given birth to a nine-pound baby girl. During the birth, Elsie got a good look at her baby in the large mirror that was suspended over her hospital bed. She could see that the baby was extremely fair in color with a head full of coal-black, curly hair.

"It's a girl, Mrs. Smith," the doctor announced as he handed the child off to the nurse.

Even though Elsie had assumed she'd have another boy, as did both friends and family because of Elsie's masculine track record, she was pleasantly surprised she'd birthed a daughter. After a thorough cleaning, Baby Girl Smith was wrapped in a white hospital blanket and held up in front of her mother.

"She's beautiful," Elsie whispered before drifting off into a sound sleep.

The next morning, Elsie found herself in a four-bed hospital room with another black woman and two white women. Coincidently, the other black woman was also named Smith.

In the morning when the nurses arrived in the room with the babies, all the women sat up in preparation for feeding. When the nurse handed Elsie a little chestnut-colored, bald-headed baby, she knew something was not right. She looked across the room at the other Mrs. Smith, who was nursing a baby with a full head of coal-black hair.

This is not my baby, Elsie thought.

She sprang into action. She gently opened the diaper of the precious but misplaced baby in her arms. The wee little male appendage staring up at her confirmed her suspicion.

I knew it, she thought.

Elsie began to push the nurse's call button repeatedly.

When two nurses arrived, Elsie said, "That's my baby," and pointed to the child on the breast of the other black Mrs. Smith. "I had a girl," she continued, "and this is a baby boy."

One nurse checked Elsie's wristband and then checked the band on the ankle of the baby she was holding. The nurse's eyes widened, and her dark skin turned gray.

"Go get the charge nurse," the one nurse ordered the other.

When the head nurse, who was in charge, arrived and was briefed about the mix-up, she began apologizing profusely. "Mrs. Smith, please know that this type of thing has never happened here. We are so sorry."

"It's okay," Elsie said interrupting the charge nurse. "I have no intentions of lodging a complaint. Just give me my baby."

"Yes ma'am," the charge nurse replied, scooping the baby boy from Elsie's arms while the attending nurse pried Elsie's baby girl from the reluctant other Mrs. Smith's arms.

After the nurses left the room, the two Mrs. Smith's began to talk about the incident.

"Listen," the mother of the baby boy said. "Does your husband know you had a girl?"

"No," Elsie replied looking curiously at the petite, brown-skinned woman, wondering where her line of questioning was about to lead.

"Now, you said you have two boys already and was expecting

to have another boy, right?" The woman didn't wait for a response. "Well," she continued while walking over to Elsie's side of the room with her baby and settling down in the bedside chair by Elsie, "I also have two boys, but I really want a daughter."

"So?" Elsie said bracing for what words would come next.

"So … we can switch babies, and no one would suspect a thing." The woman scooted her chair closer to Elsie's bed. "Look. You told me everyone gave you blue baby clothes because y'all thought you were having another boy. I have all this pink and yellow stuff 'cause I thought I'd be having a girl. C'mon, let's switch. What do you say?"

Elsie blinked. *Am I dreaming? Surely this has to be a joke*, she thought.

Although she felt bad for the desperate woman, Elsie wasn't about to swap out her beautiful child for someone else's, be they girl or boy.

"No, I can't do that," Elsie finally responded.

Elsie remained composed. Her ward mate might be suffering from any number of physiological impairments where trading in her spanking brand-new son for a perfect little female stranger seemed sane and even logical. No. Elsie would not rile this woman, but she'd give her a look as emphatic as hell. The other Mrs. Smith looked into Elsie's eyes and got the message. She slinked back to her bed with her own baby.

* * *

The following Wednesday was Valentine's Day. All the mothers, including Elsie, were sitting up in their beds wearing their finest gowns and bed jackets. Elsie's roommates bragged about what their husbands would bring them that day. Though dressed for the part, Elsie didn't dare bank on Fred remembering to buy flowers or candy for her on Valentine's Day or any occasion. He hadn't even been in to visit Elsie since she gave birth days ago. Fred didn't even know he had a baby girl.

Though Elsie knew Fred wouldn't show, she still felt like such a fool when her husband was the only one who was AWOL for Valentine's Day.

How did I end up married to Fred? She thought, stewing at her predicament.

At thirty years old, Elsie and Fred had now been married for almost eight years. She remembered that all of her friends in Florida had married years before she had and had already had two or three children by the time they had been twenty-one.

I guess I just wanted to be married like everyone else, she thought.

In Elsie's community, if you weren't married by eighteen, people would start calling you an old maid or a spinster.

She recalled the time when Fred told her that she had won out over two other women he had considered marrying. One had been two years younger than Elsie and had lived two blocks from her in Pensacola. The other had lived in Montgomery, Alabama, about two hours away. Fred used to refer to her as "Miss Montgomery."

"Miss Montgomery was a close second," Fred said.

At the time, this had made the young and naive Elsie feel special—like she had been the best, most special, and first choice. Now lying in the hospital, after giving birth to their third child, Elsie simply felt duped—like the winner of an outrageous booby prize.

Her mind drifted to her two boys. Rodney and John were crazy about Fred.

Fred lets them do whatever they want when he's drunk, she thought.

They didn't know that it was Elsie who bought their birthday and Christmas presents and told them it was from their father. She made Fred look good in the boys' eyes. However, Fred did not deserve it. Elsie covered a multitude of Fred's faults for the sake of her boys. She sighed and closed her eyes.

I wish the hell he had went on with Miss Montgomery, she thought before drifting off to sleep.

Chapter 4

Fred entered the dry cleaner's at Bolling Air Force Base to pick up his uniforms. As he flung open the door, the sound of a cowbell rang out. Cathy, the store clerk, emerged from the back room to greet her customer.

"Well, hello, Sergeant Smith," she said. "How are you today?"

"I'm doing all right," Fred replied while handing her his claim ticket. She tapped the overhead lever that caused the conveyor belt to turn.

"So, did your wife have the baby yet?"

"I don't know."

"What do you mean you don't know? Is she in the hospital?"

"Yeah. We took her in Sunday night."

"Sunday night," Cathy exclaimed as she pulled his uniforms off the conveyer rack. "Today is Thursday," she continued. "Here," she said, pulling the telephone from under the counter. Call the hospital and check up on your wife's condition."

Fred pulled out his wallet and paid for his dry cleaning and then called the hospital. "Hello. This is Sergeant John F. Smith. I'm calling about my wife, Elsie Smith. She was brought into the maternity ward on Sunday."

"Yes, Sergeant Smith," the voice on the other end of the phone replied. "Congratulations! You have a bouncing baby girl."

"A girl," Fred exclaimed. "Thanks." Fred hung up the phone.

"Well I think you had better get to the hospital now to meet your daughter," Cathy said.

She held back her judgment, but Fred could feel her thinking how shameful it was that he hadn't inquired about his wife before now. Fred couldn't explain his actions himself.

* * *

Elsie heard Fred tiptoe into her hospital room. Visiting hours would be over in an hour. Her back was turned to the door, but she could smell the liquor as he approached.

"Psst," Fred hissed trying to get Elsie's attention.

Elsie cringed. She rolled over and saw him looking a mess—a disgrace to the air force uniform. His pants were twisted in an attempt to hide the urine stain, which had happened when he had been drinking after work and couldn't make it to the toilet in time. The brim of his cap was sideways—a look she despised.

"Hello there little momma," Fred said to Elsie.

"Where have you been all this time? The baby was born on Sunday. It's a girl by the way."

"I know. Cathy from the cleaners told me to call. I just found out it's a girl."

Elsie sucked her teeth, rolled her eyes, and shook her head.

"The dry cleaning lady had to tell you to call to inquire about your own child?"

"Now Momma, don't be mad," Fred said in the condescending tone that Elsie hated.

He sometimes spoke to her as if she was a child. Fred was eighteen years older than Elsie. They married when Elsie was twenty-two and Fred was forty. Fred had taken care of Elsie and the boys, and she didn't have to work. She was totally dependent on him. But now, thirty-year-old Elsie craved freedom and independence from the forty-eight-year-old Fred.

"Visiting hours will be over soon. You had better get over to the nursery if you want to see the baby," she said. "You can't miss her. She's the only one with a head full of hair."

Elsie recalled that Fred could be really mean when it came to black folk's hair. There were some little girls in their old neighborhood with short, kinky hair. Fred couldn't stand those kids and used to call them "clinker tops," referring to their uncombed, matted hair. He used to say, "Elsie, if you ever have a girl, she better not be a clinker top."

"Okay, I'll go see her now," Fred said, interrupting Elsie's thoughts.

When he arrived at the nursery, he tapped on the window to get the nurse's attention. He folded his arms as if he was holding an imaginary baby.

The nurse mouthed, "Which one?"

Fred pointed in the direction of his newborn and mouthed "Baby Girl Smith."

The nurse held the baby up to the glass so that Fred could see his big bundle of joy. He plastered a goofy smile on his face while tapping on the glass and saying, "Hey there, Babby."

* * *

Rodney and John could hardly contain their excitement as they walked behind Fred down the long sterile halls at Malcolm Grow Medical Center. They giggled while holding their hands to their mouths to muffle the sound.

"Quiet," Fred whispered, looking over his shoulder at the boys while holding his index finger to his lips. "You're not supposed to be here."

As the trio continued to walk the narrow hall lined with highly hung portraits of various air force generals whose eyes seemed to follow their every move, they approached a lone window cut out of the wall where a night nurse sat. Fred motioned for the boys to get down onto the floor and quietly low crawl past the nurse's window while he distracted her.

"Good evening ma'am," Fred said. He was off military duty but was still wearing his uniform.

"Good evening, Sergeant Smith," the nurse responded, noticing his rank insignia on his upper arm and last name on his breast pocket.

"Say, is there a restroom down this hall?" He pointed toward the left. The boys had cleared the window without the nurse's notice and had taken off for the ward.

"Yes, Sergeant Smith. It's just a little further down on the right."

"Thanks."

Fred caught up with the boys, and they navigated their way to the maternity ward. The boys had bugged Fred about seeing their new sister ever since he told them that they had finally had one.

Before he allowed the boys to step in front of the large glass window of the nursery, Fred ensured that the coast was clear. He craned his neck in both directions and then smashed his nose against the glass. When he confirmed that the nurse was not inside the nursery, Fred lifted John up so he could see the baby.

"She's right there on the end of the second row. You see Baby Girl Smith?"

"Yeah, I see her," John squealed.

"Shh. Not so loud. Can you see her, Rodney?" Fred asked his oldest son who stood on tiptoe.

"Yeah, I see her. She's looks white."

"Excuse me," a voice from behind said, startling Fred, who immediately dropped John down to his feet.

"What are you doing here with these children?" The nursery nurse sounded like a serious lady, and the scowl on her face confirmed it.

"Aw, the boys just wanted to see their little sister, that's all."

"Sergeant Smith, you know children are not allowed in the maternity ward. Now out, all of you.

* * *

Elsie was finally released from the hospital on Wednesday, February 21, 1962. A snowstorm had slammed into the city and had caused a delay in her discharge. Fred arrived at the hospital drunk. Elsie was uncomfortable with his driving her and their newborn home, but what other choice did she have?

Dear God, please get us home safely, she prayed silently.

The ride home was quiet and unremarkable. Elsie wanted Fred to pay attention to his driving so she decided not to talk. However, the silence was broken when Fred glanced over and looked at the fair-skinned baby who had one eye opened and the other eye closed.

"She looks like one of those poor white Hoosiers from Georgia, peeping with one eye open," Fred said, snickering like a hyena.

Elsie cut her eyes over to Fred and frowned at him for several seconds. Fred, totally oblivious, continued to snicker to himself.

Fred can say the most ignorant things, especially when he's drunk, Elsie thought.

When they arrived home and entered the house, Elsie stopped dead in her tracks. The house was an absolute mess. For the ten days she was in the hospital, no one had lifted a finger to do any housecleaning. Elsie looked around the living room. Food, clothes, shoes and dirty dishes littered the floor. Still holding the baby, she entered the kitchen to find dishes piled up in the sink, dirty pots and pans on the stove, and greasy handprints on the refrigerator door. In the bathroom, the toilet bowel contained caked-on feces. Elsie nearly puked.

Couldn't they even bother to flush after themselves?

Elsie backed out of the room. She walked down the short hall to the boys' room and opened the door.

Oh my God, she gasped.

The white spreads on the boys' twin beds had dirty footprints all over them. The ceiling above the beds showed a pattern of dirty handprints. *It's like they just jumped up and down on the beds with dirty shoes on and hit the ceiling with their filthy hands,* Elsie thought.

She shook with fury. She turned on her heels and walked back down the hall to the master bedroom. The bed was unmade, which was no surprise, but it smelled like Fred had passed out on it and peed a few times. Elsie jerked her head around to where the baby's crib was set up.

"I'll be damned," she said out loud. *The damn bed is put together ass backwards. I'm gonna kill him,* Elsie shrieked inside herself.

She stormed to the living room to confront Fred about the entire mess he'd made of everything, but Fred was nowhere to be found. Elsie ran to the window and looked outside. Fred's car was gone. She knew the boys were down the street playing with the redheaded brothers. Exhausted, overwhelmed, and ready to cry, Elsie called her good friend Lillian Hardy.

"Hello," Lillian answered on the other end of the line.

"Lillian, I'm home with the baby. The house is a mess. Food and dishes are everywhere. The boys' beds looks like they've been jumping on them with their muddy shoes on. And the bathroom," she paused, "shit is all caked up in the toilet. They couldn't even be bothered with flushing the damn toilet," she shrieked, her voice cracking while tears streamed down her face.

"It's okay Elsie. Just sit tight. I'll be right over," Lillian reassured.

"Sit? I can't sit anywhere in this filthy house. I can't even lay the baby down in the crib because Fred put it up ass backwards."

"Everything will be fine. I'm on my way."

Lillian arrived twenty minutes later to find Elsie and the baby perched on the arm of the sofa. It appeared to be the cleanest place in the house.

Lillian revved into action. She began by reassembling the crib. Fred had the headboard facing in the opposite direction, and the spring mattress support was not level. Once the baby was settled in her crib, Lillian stripped all the beds and put on clean sheets, blankets, and pillow cases. She gathered and washed all the dirty dishes, pots, and pans as well as wiping down the refrigerator.

The bathroom was the challenge. There was no toilet brush or rubber gloves so Lillian began by flushing the toilet multiple times. Then she wrapped her right hand with an old towel and scrubbed the toilet bowl. She removed the caked-on feces and flushed several more times in between. Elsie watched her friend from the bathroom door.

I'm not sure I would scrub her toilet like this, Elsie thought. *I will always be a friend to Lillian,* she vowed.

Elsie's mind went back to Fred. She wondered how he could just let the boys run wild like that and totally demolish the house. *He had to be drunk the whole time,* she surmised.

Fred had proven, many times over the years, he could not be relied upon or depended on. She wondered how she had ended up with this man, who was eighteen years her senior, a heavy drinker, and a smoker.

Fred was just like her father, Sam Underwood, whom she had loved but had despised because of his drinking as well. At a very young age, Elsie had found herself taking charge of the household expenses. Every payday, she cashed her father's check, paid all the bills, bought the groceries, and would give him whatever monies was leftover.

Sam had often made promises to Elsie that he hadn't kept. For instance, because she had had narrow feet, regular shoes had not fit her feet very well. Sam had often promised to take Elsie to the French Bootery, which had been a store that specialized in narrow-sized shoes, and let her pick any pair she'd liked.

Of course, each time she had reminded him of his promise, his drunkard reply had been, "Shit! I'm not paying five dollars for one pair of shoes."

Elsie hated herself for marrying a man so much like her father, but isn't that what people said little girls always did ... married their daddies? She had experienced many broken promises and disappointments from her father, and the cycle was repeating with Fred. Now she wondered if she had sentenced her sleeping baby girl, in the next room, to the same fate.

Chapter 5

Baby Liz was queen of the house. Her brothers catered to her every whimper, from preparing her bottle in the wee hours of the morning, to tiptoeing into their parents' room and taking turns holding the bottle to the fussy baby's mouth. They enjoyed their baby sister. One such early morning, Elsie awoke to the sound of the boys arguing about whose turn it was to hold the bottle.

"Boys, what are you doing up? Go back to bed. You have school in the morning. I'll take care of the baby," Elsie said.

The boys exited the room in lockstep and returned to their beds. Elsie realized that John and Rodney were in tune to the precise time Liz would awake for a feeding and would come with a bottle before she started to cry.

What she really needs is to be changed, Elsie thought, smiling to herself at the boys' devotion to their baby sister.

She remembered the day they all sat down to decide what to name the baby since Paul Anthony Smith was not going to work for a girl.

"Let's name her Alethia Elmira after my aunt," Fred suggested.

Fred's aunt was an intelligent, sophisticated, and educated woman living in New York, of whom he was most proud. She was married but had no children. Fred secretly believed that his daughter would gain a financial benefit in the future if she was his aunt's namesake. Although that did not occur, he unwittingly drew a prophetic parallel between Baby Liz and her great-aunt in that she would grow up to be an intelligent, educated woman. And like her great-aunt, she would marry late in life and would bear no children.

"No, Fred. I'm sorry. I don't like that name," Elsie protested.

Fred was disappointed by Elsie's flat-out rejection of the name. But his persistence didn't waiver.

"Okay. How about after my mother, Dora Elizabeth?"

"Elizabeth is okay, but I don't really like the name Dora either. It reminds me of a girl I knew back in Pensacola who was dumber than a box of rocks. We called her 'Dumb Dora'."

Fred stared at Elsie for a few seconds in disbelief that she would compare his mother's name with someone she considered dumb.

"Dumb Dora couldn't spell worth a damn either," Elsie continued. "The teacher would ask her to spell cat, and she would look up into the air and start with the letter M."

Elsie laughed at the memory. Fred became impatient with Elsie's jesting. He was being serious.

Still trying to honor is aunt, Fred made another suggestion. "Okay, what about Elizabeth Elmira?"

Elsie shot Fred a cross look. Before she could shoot him down again, John interjected a suggestion. "How about Marie for the middle name, after you, Elsie?"

Elsie's eyes widened.

"Elizabeth Marie Smith," Elsie repeated. "Okay, now we're talking. It's settled."

Fred sighed, feeling defeated.

Well at least she's partially named after my mother, he thought.

"Okay, I'll buy that," Fred replied in a solemn tone.

* * *

John often mocked the name Elizabeth.

"It sounds like lizard," he joked, sticking out his tongue and making a slurping sound like a reptile.

John did not know that his sister would later endure taunts from her elementary school classmates about her name, who often called her "lizard" or "Gila monster." However, this cruel name twisting did not last beyond elementary school. The nickname that John would saddle his sister with for life was one that she grew to hate with each passing year.

When Baby Liz started talking, she called John "Don" and Rodney "Nodney." For the sake of their little sister, John and Rodney decided to stop calling their parents "Elsie" and "Fred" and to start calling them "Mama" and "Daddy." One day John tried teaching his baby sister how to say her own name.

"Say Bet-Bet," John said in his version of baby talk. Liz ignored him. "Beth-Beth," John continued. She continued to ignore him. Finally, he said, "Becky."

Liz looked up at him, and John determined that it was the name she preferred to be called. The rest of the family followed suit, and the nickname stuck. The nickname would prove to be a sore spot for Liz, and she struggled with her family for her own identity for many years.

* * *

Fred stumbled into the house just before midnight. He had been drinking at a local bar near the base. He and his cronies had closed the place. Now at home and still in a talkative mood, Fred decided to check on the boys.

"Psst," Fred said peeking into Rodney and John's room. "Y'all up?"

After getting no response, Fred tiptoed into the room and turned on the table lamp.

"Hey," he said with a loud whispered voice while shaking each boy's bed. "Y'all awake?" He asked.

"We are now," John replied, sitting up and rubbing his eyes.

Fred reeked of alcohol as he stumbled across the room taking a seat at the boys' desk. He crossed one leg over the other and began telling the boys stories from his World War II days when he had first joined the army in 1943. He also talked about his time in Japan when he had been deployed just months before John had been born, and how he had sent a list of Japanese names to Elsie to consider naming John. But she had decided to name her baby John after his father, Fred's given name, in the event Fred didn't return from the war.

The boys had heard these stories a million times. Fred had told them the same way every time. They had heard the stories so often they could repeat them verbatim. What they hated most about these times was that Fred never really had much to say to them until he was drunk.

Fred began to tell the story about when he had returned from Japan and Rodney had not remembered him. He said that one day he had spanked Rodney for messing his pants. Rodney had been furious and had run to Elsie to complain. "That old boy hit me," Rodney had cried.

Fred laughed as he recounted the story again to his sons before nodding off to sleep still sitting in the chair at the boys' desk. His leg was still crossed over the other one. John switched off the lamp, and he and Rodney went back to sleep.

As an adult, John and his wife, Celeste, were drug users. They had two children, Tony and Yavonne. John despised Celeste when she would get high and then want to hold the children hostage with her foolish drug-induced conversation. She'd then nod off to sleep in front of them.

Why would she do that to the kids? John said, recalling these incidents. He never seemed to recognize the irony that he had essentially married someone like his father.

Chapter 6

SUMMER 1964

Fred drove Rodney and John to the baseball field on Bolling Air Force Base on a hot Saturday afternoon in late June. It would be the boys' first game playing with the base team. Coach Roddybush was one of Fred's coworkers. After a couple of brothers had to quit the team when their father had been stationed to Fort Bragg in North Carolina, the coach had asked Fred if his boys would be interested in playing on the team. The coach even allowed Rodney and John to join them without trying out.

Fred loved baseball. He was a big fan of the old Negro leagues and admired players like Satchel Paige. In 1956, when he had transferred from Eglin Air Force Base in Pensacola, Florida, to Bolling Air Force Base in Washington, DC, Fred had enjoyed attending a few of the Washington Senators baseball games at Griffin Stadium.

"Y'all enjoy yourselves," Fred said as the boys hopped out of the car.

"Ain't you going to stay and watch?" John asked.

"Naw. Y'all go on and have fun. You can get the team bus back home."

Rodney turned unfazed and headed toward the field. John lingered, watching Fred drive off before joining his brother.

The irony of Fred loving the game of baseball but failing to watch his sons play one single game was not lost on Rodney and John. Fred spent his entire summer leisure time listening to baseball games broadcasted on the radio. He even used a legal-sized ledger to record the scores and innings.

"Why you think Daddy didn't stay to watch the game?" John asked Rodney as they walked the two miles back home because they had opted not to ride the team bus.

"It don't matter," Rodney said. "Nobody's parents come to watch. Anyway, do you really want Daddy to be there?"

"Naw. I guess not," John said punching his hand in his baseball glove.

Deep down John knew Rodney was right. Fred's drunkenness was embarrassing, but Fred was their primary male role model whom they looked to for cues on how a man should behave.

Fred always had a plastic cup full of gin and orange juice. John called this "Fred's Cup of Courage." He recalled how he sometimes sat on the front stoop of their house with Fred. When a car drove down the street faster than the posted speed limit, Fred would yell at the driver, "Hey, slow that car down."

Sometimes John thought this was funny. He knew if his father wasn't lit up, he'd never have the nerve to be so bold.

One day, somebody's gonna stop and kick Daddy's skinny butt, John thought.

He also drew comparisons between Fred and other fathers. Their friend and neighbor, Jerry Croom's father was shorter than Fred was but much more muscular. Jerry and John were in the same class at school. Jerry had a propensity for leaning back in his chair with the front legs of the chair off the floor. John remembered the day their white, male teacher had kicked Jerry's chair causing him to fall backward. The following day, Mr. Croom had come to school to confront the teacher for his actions.

"Man, if you ever do that again, I'm gonna break my foot off in your ass," Mr. Croom could be heard yelling from the hall.

Now that's what a father should be, John thought.

Jerry Croom was loved and protected. It wasn't that John didn't feel wanted by his father. He guessed that Fred loved him in his own way. But John wanted Jerry Croom's father's kind of love from Fred.

The boys entered the house through the back door. Elsie was in the kitchen frying fish.

"We won our game." John beamed looking up at his mother.

"That's good," Elsie said smiling. "Did y'all have a good time?"

"Yes, it was fun."

"Well, y'all need to go wash up for dinner. You smell like dogs that's been rolling around in the grass."

Both boys laughed.

"Okay," they said.

When they exited the kitchen into the living room, Fred was on the sofa. They paused for a moment and looked at him. He was sitting up, but he was passed out drunk.

"C'mon, let's go," Rodney said, leaving John still standing in the living room.

John noticed the urine stain on the front of Fred's pants. The boys saw their father passed out on the sofa with pissed pants on a recurring basis. Rodney was numb to it and ignored Fred. But John couldn't. It bothered him. He wanted Fred to be a normal father like Mr. Croom.

"Daddy, we won our game," John said.

Fred didn't respond.

"Daddy did you hear me?"

Fred lifted his head. His eyes were narrow slits.

"Huh?" Fred said groggily.

"I said we won our game," John repeated.

Fred lowered his head once again. John craned his neck in an attempt to see Fred's face. It was useless. Fred had conked out again.

SUMMER 1971

Liz's earliest toddler memory of her father was of her lying face up on her back with her feet resting on Fred's shoulders. He would lift his heels off the floor causing a gentle rocking motion that soothed her.

She remembered him waking her in the morning and carrying her into the kitchen where her mother would be preparing breakfast. She'd have her head resting on Fred's shoulder. He would turn his back toward his wife so mother and daughter faced one another.

"Good morning mama," Fred would say on behalf of the still sleepy little girl.

She also remembered greeting her father every day when he had picked her up from the Bolling Air Force Base nursery.

"Daddy, Daddy, Daddy," she had squealed when she saw him enter the room that was full of children waiting for their parents' arrivals.

With full force, she raced toward him and paused just long enough to take a flying leap into his outreached arms. The catch came with such force that it had literally caused Fred to swing around 180 degrees. The impact such a force would have had on her fifty-two-year-old father's body had never crossed little Liz's mind.

As she had gotten older, she had longed for those earlier days when she had been blissfully ignorant of her father's vices. During the summer of 1971, when Liz was nine, she often sat on the front porch of their house with her father. Fred sat in his web chaise lounge chair and listened to baseball games on the radio. He had his pad and pencil and would create his own scoreboard.

Liz hadn't really cared for sports but had tried to muster interest in order to spend time and to have something in common with Fred. She had found herself becoming somewhat of a chameleon—a type of lizard her brother John had first teased that her name sounded like. She had people-pleased with her brothers too. If the boys had liked moon pies, she had eaten them too, even though she had hated the marshmallow center.

"So what's an RBI," Liz asked, glancing at the notepad Fred wrote on to keep the statistics of the game.

"Runs batted in," Fred answered quickly without raising his eyes from the pad. His response told her no more than she had known five seconds before that, but she decided not to ask the obvious follow up question: So what does runs batted in mean?

"Will you bring me an orange juice?" he asked Liz without taking a breath.

"Sure," she said. Liz rose from her chair and entered the house. After staring in the refrigerator for a few seconds, she retrieved an eight-ounce can of unsweetened Donald Duck brand orange juice. No one in the house liked this brand of orange juice. Fred bought it to mix with his Smirnoff gin, which he often bought by the pint.

"Here, daddy," Liz said, handing him the can.

"Thank you, Babby."

Usually when Fred was drinking, he would engage in conversation for hours. She noticed that her father was not very talkative until he was drinking. His affinity to the sport of baseball was something that he enjoyed alone, so she was starting to feel like she was intruding.

This seemed odd to her because people who enjoyed watching sports generally did so with friends. But her father really didn't have any friends. An introvert for the most part, Fred did not entertain other men in his home. On occasion, he hung out with Lillian Hardy's husband, Leroy, at their home when the two families got together. But like Fred, Leroy was also a drinker. At times, Fred socialized with the neighbors, Mr. Jones who lived across the street or Mr. Edison who lived two doors down. But again, these men drank, and drinking was the only thing they all had in common.

WASHINGTON, DC

1972

On a cool spring day in April 1972, ten-year-old Liz sat in attendance in her fifth-grade class at Congress Heights Elementary when she heard two of her classmates giggling in the back of the room.

"Somebody's drunk granddaddy is here," she heard one say.

Liz took a quick glance over her right shoulder and saw that it was her father standing in the hall with a baseball cap cocked to one side of his head—a look that she hated. Fred was trying to get the teacher's attention. Embarrassed, Liz felt knots forming in the pit of her stomach. She wanted to go under her desk. Better yet, she wanted to just disappear.

"Miss McNair, someone is here to see you," a student sitting near the door said.

The teacher excused herself and stepped outside the classroom.

"Whose father is that?" One student asked aloud.

Liz did not want to acknowledge that it was her father. First of all, kids teased you if you had a drunk parent or a fat parent, and it certainly was not cool to have an older parent. Liz struck out on all three counts. She had both an older dad who drank and an overweight mother.

"Elizabeth," Miss McNair called, sticking her head back into the room. "Will you step out into the hall for a minute? Your father needs to speak with you."

The kids in the back of the class who were trying to guess whose parent was in the hall roared with laughter, pointing at Liz.

As she walked toward the door, she avoided making eye contact with her peers.

"Quiet, class," Miss McNair scolded and then returned to her lesson.

"What is it daddy?" Liz asked in a flat tone. "Why are you here?"

"I accidently locked myself out of the house. May I borrow your key?" Liz released a heavy sigh.

How in the hell did you lock yourself out? She screamed in her head.

Liz removed the key that was tied to a long piece of mauve-colored ribbon, which hung around her neck.

"Here." Liz held a stiffened arm out before her as the key swung left and right on the ribbon.

"Thanks, Babby," Fred replied taking the key and turning to leave.

"Babby," she mumbled after sucking her teeth. *He never says Baby but always Babby*, she thought.

Reluctant to return to the classroom, Liz watched as Fred made his way down the corridor, weaving a little from side to side.

When he turned the corner to enter the stairwell she thought, *just don't lose my key on the way back home.*

When she returned to class, she caught the eye of a couple of classmates who were obviously still enjoying the spectacle. One boy taunted her by turning his hand toward his mouth, crossing his eyes, and sticking his tongue out to the side in an attempt at mimicking a drunk person.

Liz prayed silently, *Why me Lord?*

Chapter 7

During the summer of 1973, eleven-year-old Liz got into the habit of staying up late and listening to music on the stereo through the headphones her brother Rodney had left her when he and John had joined the army the previous year. One night, she sat on the living room sofa in total darkness listening to Michael Jackson's first solo album, *Got to Be There*. It was thirty-five minutes of pure bubblegum R & B soul music. She loved each and every song on the album and played it over and over in its entirety.

Songs like "I Wanna Be Where You Are" and "Wings of My Love" caused Liz to feel trepidation. A trembling motion in her stomach occurred when she wondered if anyone would ever feel so passionately about her. She tried to image her future and what it would be like—when and who she would marry and how many children she would have. But her daydreams were often hazy. She really couldn't imagine the man of her dreams. So instead, in her mind, she pretended that she was different. She conjured up an image of herself as the extroverted and multi-talented singer, songwriter, and dancer girlfriend of Michael Jackson, living in Encino, California.

At about a quarter to midnight, she was pulled from her fantasy world when she saw a tall thin shadow enter the living room and move toward the front door. It was Fred. He didn't see her. She removed the headphones and called out to him in a loud whisper.

"Hey, daddy," she said, startling her father who had just reached for the doorknob.

"Shit! You scared me," he said.

Liz turned on the table lamp to see Fred, his eyes wide with surprise.

What are you still doing up at this time of night?"

"I'm listening to music. Where are you going this time of night?" Liz smirked and peered at her father.

"I'm going to the store."

Fred gave Liz a challenging look, though his shoulders slouched. He knew he was busted, and he knew that Liz knew it too. Their eyes stayed locked on each other for a few seconds. Liz narrowed her eyes, and then Fred finally blinked. In this moment, Liz somehow knew she had the upper hand, and it gave her a sense of power.

"Well bring me back some Pixy Stix," she demanded.

"They don't have that sort of thing at this store," Fred said in exasperation, growing impatient.

"Well, do they have potato chips?" Liz snapped back.

She had developed a hankering for sweet and salty snacks. She unconsciously used food to soothe her innate feelings of inadequacy. Although she was currently in fantasy mode where she usually felt good about herself, she decided to seize the opportunity that had unexpectedly presented itself.

"Yes, they have potato chips," Fred huffed.

"What about fruit punch soda? Do they sell that?"

"I think so, yes."

"Okay, then bring me back some Bon Ton Bar-B-Q potato chips and a bottle of Tahitian Treat Fruit Punch soda," Liz said.

Fred rolled his eyes and left for the liquor store. Liquor was not sold on Sunday, but Fred knew of a few liquor stores in Maryland that began selling hard liquor at the stroke of midnight.

Liz had busted her father sneaking out of the house that night to buy booze. For her silence, he would have to pay the price. And so each time after this night that he attempted to sneak out to make a Sunday-at-midnight, liquor run, Liz would waylay Fred and demand that he bring her something as well.

One night Fred thought he'd gotten past his daughter's toll tax. She had been in her bedroom and not the living room. He had made it out of the yard and to his car and had thought he was home free.

Lifting her bedroom window, which faced the front of the house, Liz stage-whispered, "Don't forget the potato chips and fruit punch soda."

* * *

For the remainder of the summer, Liz passed the days watching late night television, listening to music until the wee hours of the morning, sleeping until noon, and then riding her bike around the neighborhood all afternoon with her next-door neighbor Sheila. Sheila was a mildly retarded white girl, who was three years older than Liz.

One day in late August after riding bikes in the heat all afternoon, Liz brought Sheila back to her house to get a cold soft drink. When they entered the dining room, they both stopped dead in their tracks. There lay Fred sprawled out at the bottom of the staircase landing passed out.

"Mr. Smith," Sheila called, scared that Fred either fell down the stairs, was hurt, or even worse, was dead.

Liz stood stoically looking at her father for several seconds. She wasn't worried that he might have fallen or been hurt. She squinted, disgusted at the sight of him, and then blinked as if she were trying to snap herself out of a trance. She grabbed Sheila's hand for a brief moment and gave it a little squeeze.

"It's okay," Liz said in an effort to calm Sheila's fears.

Though embarrassed, Liz didn't let on to Sheila but instead forced herself to act as normal as possible while rousing her father. Liz had gotten proficient at playing cool, calm, and collected. It was a metaphoric mask she wore when she was embarrassed by her father. She would later learn to use humor to hide the embarrassment, pain, and disappointment Fred caused.

"Daddy," she said repeatedly until Fred opened his eyes.

"Yeah, what?" Fred answered in a groggy state.

"Let's get you upstairs," Liz said in a matter-of-fact tone of voice.

She helped her father to his feet and led him up the narrow staircase. Sometimes Liz felt like she was the parent. Once upstairs in his bedroom, Fred plopped onto the bed facedown and didn't utter another word. Liz returned downstairs to see Sheila standing in the same spot still looking concerned.

"Is he all right?" Sheila asked.

"Yeah, he's fine," Liz said flippantly and waved her hand in a dismissive motion.

Liz learned to put up an emotional wall around her heart and tried not to let the shame of having an alcohol abuser for a father bother her. She was relieved that it was Sheila who had witnessed Fred passed out on the stairs opposed to another playmate. Sheila could relate to having a drunk parent because her mother stayed tanked up all the time.

"So, what kind of soda do you want," Liz asked Sheila, refusing to be humiliated. She found it easier to block out her true feelings and to focus on the trivial. "We have cola, orange, grape, and root beer."

"I'll have a root beer," Sheila stammered, taking Liz's lead and moving past the incident. After this episode, Liz was always anxious about having her friends around the house when her father was home.

Chapter 8

Liz was thirteen in 1975 when her maternal grandfather, Sam Underwood, died. She and her mother made the twenty-two-hour trip to Pensacola, Florida, by Greyhound bus, to attend the service. Fred took them to the bus station and was advised of the date and time that they would return.

The funeral was in September, and Liz missed several days of school in order to accompany her mother on the trip. Once in Pensacola, Elsie took over the responsibility of funeral arrangements. The service was held on a beautiful fall afternoon in Sam's home church with an abundance of mourners, including his older sister, Nanny, now his only surviving sibling.

"My baby brother," Nanny cried.

Liz watched her mother cringe and shake her head as ushers carried grief-stricken Aunt Nanny out of the church. Liz knew that her mother believed Nanny was merely putting on an act and that her outburst didn't come from a place of sincerity.

"Why is she doing all that confounded whooping and hollering?" Elsie asked her sister Bernice in low voice.

Bernice didn't answer. She didn't even look at Elsie. She simply hunched her shoulders and fixed her eyes forward.

Nanny had been a young woman with a newborn of her own when her brother, Sam, had been born. She had even served as a wet nurse for him. Now he was dead. Years of drinking and smoking had not only cost Sam both his legs but ultimately his life.

Though it was a sad occasion, Elsie enjoyed being with her family, and Liz felt a bit relaxed too. Maybe it was because the few days they'd been away from home and from Fred, nothing embarrassing or hurtful had happened.

* * *

"Hello Fred," Elsie said on the long-distance collect call back home. "We'll be leaving Pensacola this afternoon and should arrive in DC at seven o'clock tomorrow night. I'll call you from the Greyhound station when we're back in town."

"Okay, Babby," Fred replied in the all too familiar inebriated voice. A sense of trepidation came over Elsie like a dark shadow.

Fred can't do shit without drinking, she thought.

Her mind went back to her now-deceased father. The irony and the parallels that could be drawn between Fred and her father were not lost on Elsie. Both had been drunks, and neither could be relied on nor depended on in a pinch.

The bus was delayed for two hours in Atlanta, Georgia. Elsie called the house to inform Fred about the delay. She held the receiver of the bus station's pay phone to her ear and began to bite her bottom lip after hearing the ninth ring on the other end of the line. She slammed the receiver back on its hook.

"What's the matter?" Liz asked.

"No answer," Elsie said, smoldering. "Come on. Let's get ready to board the bus. We'll try to call again during the layover in Richmond."

On the bus, Liz tucked her legs under her body and gazed out the window into the highway's total darkness. For some reason, the song, "The Highways of My Life" by the Isley Brothers began to play in her head. While thinking about the song lyrics, they haunted her, and she felt overcome with anxiety—like an animal trapped in a cage.

Moving down the highways of my life
Making sure I stay to the right
Moving down the highways of my life
So I can't be concerned with the other side of the road

Liz was the dutiful daughter in her family dynamic. She was well behaved, didn't cause any problems, was highly responsible, and always tried to please others. The boys had gotten away. They were in the army and away from family responsibilities and burdens.

Making sure I stay to the right. Yes, that's me, Liz thought. She always did the right thing. *I can't be concerned with the other side of the road where my freedom lies because I'm so busy being worried about my parents,* she screamed within herself.

Liz held a lot in. She learned to be more in tune with the feelings and needs of others, especially her parents, than of herself.

I had a chance to be free, she thought.

She recalled the time when her mother had had enough of Fred and had wanted to leave him. Liz had understood her mother's frustration but had been more overcome by the prospect of leaving Fred alone.

What will happen to him? He can't take care of himself, she had rationalized.

How many times had he fallen asleep with something cooking on the stove? Her worst fear was that he'd die in a house fire. So she had somehow convinced her mom not to leave him and had settled into the role of *lost child*—demanding little and receiving the same. To hide her pain, she often put on a metaphorical clown face and used humor to minimize the tension between her parents.

The Greyhound bus pulled into the DC depot at nine o'clock at night. Liz and her mother exited the bus, retrieved their luggage, and entered the station. Liz was tired, so she immediately sat down in front of the row of pay telephones mounted on the wall. Elsie, once again, called the house to notify Fred of their arrival but again, got no answer. Elsie was seething because her husband had not answered when she called during their layover in Richmond, Virginia, either. She picked up her suitcase and began walking toward the taxi depot located at the back of the bus station.

"Come on. Grab your suitcase," Elsie ordered at her sleepy, irritable teenager. "Let's try to get a taxi."

Liz knew that this would be a challenge. She and her mother had had many experiences attempting to get a cab home at night from evening church services only to have been told by the drivers that they wouldn't travel to what they had called "far southeast" Washington at night. They had soon learned that the only cab company willing to travel over the Anacostia River had been the DC Yellow Top Cab Company. When they exited the building they were disappointed to see only one taxicab, and it wasn't a Yellow Top.

"Taxi, ma'am?" the driver asked.

"Yes, we're going to Raleigh Street, southeast," Elsie replied.

Looking less willing, the driver cast down his eyes and his voice changed to a high octave whine. "Well, I usually don't drive to far southeast neighborhoods this time of night."

"Oh," Elsie said with disappointment in her voice and her head hanging down.

Liz plopped down in frustration on her suitcase, which was standing upright. She released a heavy sigh.

"Now what we gonna do, Ma?" She asked Elsie, looking defeated. Before Elsie could respond, the taxi driver interjected.

"All right. I will take you home. Get in," he instructed.

"Thank you," a grateful Liz and Elsie said in unison.

It was ten o'clock at night when they finally arrived home. Liz carried her suitcase up the three steps leading to the porch and plunked it down hard on the wooden surface. Elsie followed suit with her door key in hand. She reached for the storm door handle and pulled, but to her surprise, the door would not budge.

"Shit," Elsie exclaimed.

"Now what?" Liz asked.

"This stupid ass has locked the storm door from the inside."

They both began pounding on the storm door in order to get Fred's attention. They had no idea what room he was in. The house was in total darkness, and not a light or the flickering of a television screen could be seen.

Liz remembered the day she and Sheila had found him on the staircase landing passed out. When she had guided him to his bed that day, he'd slept well into the night. She feared that this was a repeat event, and that she and her mother had little chance of rousing him out of his drunken slumber, especially from outside the house. But they had to try.

Liz began banging on every window around the first floor of the house. She then started throwing pebbles at her parents' bedroom window in hopes of getting his attention.

"Be careful not to break the window," Elsie warned.

Frustrated, Liz paused from exhaustion and placed her hands on her hips. Looking up at the bedroom window, her eyes widened when she noticed the gutter downspout. The idea struck her to bang on it.

"Give me your keys," she said to her mother.

Elsie handed over her keys, and Liz began striking the set of keys against the downspout creating an awful clanging sound, which was sure to wake the dead as well as a few of the neighbors. After a few minutes, a light finally came on from the upstairs bedroom. Fred peered down from the open window to see two shadowed figures in the backyard.

"Open the damn door," Elsie yelled. "We've been out here for the longest time."

Fred made his way downstairs and opened the front door. He then unlocked the storm door.

Not realizing his actions, he asked in a drunken stupor, "Didn't you have your key?"

"Yes, I have my key," Elsie yelled pushing past Fred to enter the living room. "You had the damn storm door locked."

"Yeah! There's no key to the storm door," Liz added, also pushing past Fred and walking in lockstep behind her mother.

"Sorry, Babby," Fred said.

Liz shook her head slightly, and a growling noise came from deep within the pit of her stomach. His pitiful "Sorry, Babby" was not going to cut it this time. Liz had had enough.

Chapter 9

WASHINGTON, DC

Winter 1975

"Oh, my God. What the hell does she have on?" Liz heard Mona say from a couple of tables away in the school cafeteria.

Liz had finished eating and got up to empty her tray. Liz generally ignored Mona when she was showing off in front of her classmates. Liz hated confrontation and chose to avoid it when humanly possible. This was a coping mechanism she had developed from having to deal with her father's drunkenness. She couldn't understand why Mona felt the need to make her look bad in front of others.

Liz had known Mona since elementary school and had once considered her a friend. But now, looking back, she wondered if Mona was ever a friend.

The two had a lot in common. Mona was the youngest of five children and had four older brothers. Her father was in the air force, and her mother worked part-time at their elementary school. Mona lived only one street over from Liz.

Her house was one of the few Liz's mother allowed her to visit because she knew Mona's mother from the school. Mona's bedroom was like a doll museum, and Liz had been in awe of it each time she visited. Mona had a Dolls of the World collection, which had been sent to her from her father when he had been overseas. Each doll was dressed in her native garb representing countries such as Spain, Japan, France, Italy, and Mexico. The dolls were on display stands, and Liz knew to look but not to touch. She had been well trained by her mother not to gawk over things and to act as though she'd seen it all before.

Although the two girls got along well, Mona had a propensity for wanting or needing to upstage Liz. One day when she had visited Liz, Mona noticed her jigsaw puzzle of a map of the United States and had asked if she could put it together. Liz had put this puzzle together many times and was delighted to let her friend work it. At the end of the playdate, Mona's brother had arrived at the house to walk his sister home.

"Mona, it's time to go. Your brother's here," Elsie had yelled from the bottom of the stairs.

"We're coming," Liz yelled back on Mona's behalf. The two walked down the stairs, through the dining room, and into the living room where Elsie was standing at the front door. Mona walked ahead of Liz.

"See you on Monday," she said to Liz as she had glanced over her shoulder.

"Okay," Liz responded.

"Thank you, Mrs. Smith," Mona said as she approached Elsie. "Oh, I had to help Elizabeth put together that puzzle of the United States because she didn't know how," she continued.

Elsie looked perplexed as Mona exited the gate and had begun walking with her brother. Liz stood behind her mother, watching them as well.

"What is she talking about? I know good and damn well you can put that puzzle together by yourself," Elsie said.

Feeling uneasy, Liz had simply hunched her shoulders, turned, and walked into the kitchen to get a snack. Once again, she had turned to sugary treats when she had felt uncomfortable or perturbed.

Liz exited the cafeteria, wanting to put as much distance between her and Mona's mocking voice as fast as she could. Liz noticed, as they got older, that a split in Mona's personality formed. When it was just the two of them, they got along famously. But when the so-called cool girls were around, Mona acted differently toward Liz. It was like she was trying to make Liz look bad in order to make herself look good. Liz maintained her friendship with Mona through elementary school, but by junior high school, things would change.

* * *

In junior high, Mona befriended a girl named Brenda. Brenda didn't know Liz, but Mona thought it would be funny to put Brenda up to bumping into Liz in the hallway.

"Oops, excuse me," Brenda would say after bumping Liz's left shoulder as she passed by. Mona, not far behind, would laugh and point. The next day, the same sort of thing occurred.

"Oh, sorry," Brenda would say after stepping on the back of Liz's shoe and causing it to come off. Liz stooped down in the crowded hallway to put her shoe back on while her classmate Michelle waited with her. Liz could hear Mona's laughter fading down the long corridor.

"Why does that girl do that?" Michelle asked.

"I don't know," Liz said frustrated and annoyed. "She's just a puppet for Mona to play with. When Mona gets tired of her, she'll put her down like she does the rest of her toys."

During the winter of 1975, Liz decided to end her so-called friendship with Mona. It happened after school that day when Mona loud-talked to Liz in the cafeteria. That day in school, Liz wore a pair of brown, plaid, corduroy pants with a white long-sleeved shirt. However, since it was so cold out that day, she decided to throw on a pullover sweater. The only pullover she could find was a white sweater with small peach-colored flowers on it. She knew that the patterns clashed but had to go with it as she was running late for school. When Mona saw the outfit, she called Liz out on it and tried to make her feel ashamed.

At about seven o'clock that evening, the telephone rang. Liz's mother, who was upstairs in her bedroom, picked up the extension. A second later, she called for Liz, who was downstairs in the living room, to pick up the phone.

"Hello," Liz said, after she heard her mother hang up the upstairs extension.

"Hi, this is Mona. I just wanted to ask you if you knew how to match your clothes."

"What?" Liz asked. Mona was really beginning to get on her nerves.

"Do you know how to match your clothes?" Mona repeated in a sarcastic tone.

This little bitch has the nerve to call me at home about this shit, Liz thought. *Something that is none of her damn business. It's not like she's really concerned about my appearance, otherwise she wouldn't have been loud talking me in the cafeteria today.*

Liz grinded her teeth in anger. She recalled that this type of behavior had been Mona's method of operation since elementary school. She was what Liz referred to as a "shit starter." It was like a game to her to see what clashes she could create between people. Liz hated this about Mona. Mona was conflict incarnate, and Liz hated conflict. Liz could not stand any arguing or fighting, whether it was verbal or physical.

Liz recognized this telephone call as a fishing expedition to solicit information to be used against her at a later date. This girl was the main reason Liz wouldn't confide in other females—they couldn't be trusted to keep their mouths shut.

She recalled an ugly episode Mona had created between Liz and a girl named Carolyn. Mona had called Liz on the phone saying, "I don't like Carolyn, do you?"

"No, not really," Liz had answered, wanting to be agreeable but feeling deep down that it was the wrong response.

The next day, Carolyn had caught Liz in the girls' washroom alone.

"I heard from Mona that you said you don't like me," Carolyn had said in a harsh tone.

She stood in front of Liz with piercing eyes waiting for a response. Liz felt her head spinning.

That damn Mona and her big mouth, Liz thought, but she only had herself to blame for falling into her trap.

Tired of staring Liz down after receiving no response, Carolyn pushed Liz. Although the two girls had been similar in height and weight, Carolyn's push had barely moved Liz. However, when Liz pushed back, the force had almost knocked Carolyn off her feet. Angered by this, Carolyn swung at Liz with an openhanded slap across her left cheek.

At that point, everything for Liz had gone in slow motion. Her cheek had burned from the slap, but she had refused to place her hand to her face. Her eyes had begun to well up with tears, but she had stopped herself from crying.

You must stay strong and not show weakness, she had told herself.

She gazed back at Carolyn for what seemed like several seconds as Carolyn's gaze had appeared to show a look of uncertainty. Liz hadn't known what to do. She had not been a fighter and had hated conflict and confrontation. Her church had preached that you should turn the other cheek.

She might slap that one too, Liz had thought.

Finally, Liz broke her gaze with Carolyn and pushed past her, exiting the girls' washroom.

"May I borrow your eraser," Carolyn had whispered to Liz just an hour after their confrontation in the washroom.

Without verbally responding, Liz had handed Carolyn her block eraser. When she had finished, Carolyn handed the eraser back to Liz.

"I'm sorry," Carolyn whispered.

Liz had felt a lump in her throat. She had grappled with her decision not to strike Carolyn back in the washroom. She wondered if it had been because she felt guilty for giving Mona the ammunition to incite Carolyn or did she simply punk out.

Liz recognized that her friendship with Mona had not been a healthy one. And she refused to be the butt end of her abuse. Now with her ear to the phone, listening to yet another setup, Liz's patience with Mona had finally come to an end.

"Yes, I know how to match my clothes," Liz finally responded to Mona's anomalous question.

"How?" Mona asked.

"What?"

"Tell me, how do you match your clothes?" Mona demanded.

Liz craned her neck to the right and then to the left until she heard her it crack. She had had enough of Mona and her antics and was no longer willing to put up with them. Liz exhaled and responded with a stern tone of voice. "Listen. I don't feel you are calling me about this out of any type of concern or friendship. So I would appreciate it if you didn't call my house anymore."

Before she could hear Mona's response, Liz slammed the telephone back on the hook. Liz felt betrayed by Mona and felt good about ending their friendship. But she could never understand why Mona chose to use what she thought was a friendship to exploit her and attempt to make her appear to be some type of buffoon.

Liz learned to hate this characteristic trait in people. Just because someone is quiet, shy, or appears to be different from the rest, it shouldn't make that person a target to be picked on or made fun of. However, in instances such as this, Liz wished that she were more like her mother. Elsie had a sharp tongue and could cuss the shoes off anyone at the drop of a hat. Liz couldn't do that. She was like Fred—quiet and nonconfrontational. But unlike Fred, Liz didn't have a magic elixir in a cup to give her courage. No, Liz would find her courage as a member of an unlikely trio.

Chapter 10

Rock of Ages Church of God was a Christian congregation that believed in observing the Seventh-Day Sabbath. The premise was based on the Old Testament scripture in Exodus 20, which stated that God created heaven and earth in six days and rested on the seventh day, making the seventh day holy. So instead of meeting on Sunday, church services were held on Saturday, which technically was the last day of the week.

The quasi-Christian, Judaic, Pentecostal, Apostolic congregation believed in water baptism, speaking in tongues, and prophecy. The women didn't wear makeup. They only wore moderate jewelry such as watches or wedding bands. Their skirts and dresses hung below their knees, their heads were covered with hats, scarves, or prayer caps, and they never wore pants. Members also did not participate in what was considered a pagan holiday or ritual such as dressing up for Halloween, participating in Easter egg hunts, and putting up Christmas trees.

Elsie joined Rock of Ages in 1971, when Liz was nine years old. Liz always wanted her father to attend church with the family, but he never did. She knew that the Holy Roller churches that her mother tended to gravitate to would not appeal to her father. Even her brothers had managed to get out of going to church by this time.

By 1976, when Liz was fourteen, she was one of only three teenagers that attended Rock of Ages. The other two teenagers were the Riley sisters. Beverly was fifteen, and Theresa was sixteen. Although Liz interacted with the Riley girls, she didn't consider them to be her friends. They didn't hang out with one another outside of church, and they didn't talk on the phone.

The woman that taught the teenage Bible class was Sister Shaw. Sister Shaw was young, about twenty-six years old, and married to a minister in the church. The Shaw's were a childless couple. After a year of marriage, they had decided to take in two teenage girls through the foster care system.

Pamela was sixteen and physically disabled. She was born with a club foot, which was a congenital deformity of her right foot. She wore an elevated shoe with a brace attached and used forearm crutches for mobility.

Gerlisa was fifteen. She had a facial deformity. Her left arm was several inches shorter than her right arm, and she was mildly retarded.

In just a few months, the girls thrived in the Shaw's home and in the church. Liz, Pamela, and Gerlisa became fast friends. Liz visited them at their home on a regular basis, and Gerlisa spent several nights with Liz at her house.

In church, the Riley sisters were the shining stars. They had beautiful singing voices—especially Theresa. Theresa's signature song was "I Made a Vow to the Lord," which she sang as a solo. Theresa had a voice like you would image an angel in heaven might have. She was a full-figured, young lady, was tall and curvy, had dark mocha colored skin, and large dark sparkling eyes. She and her sister Beverly often sang together at various churches as a duet. Their signature song together was called "The Potter." Liz loved to hear the harmony between the sisters: Theresa sang in the upper ranges, and Beverly sang in the lower ranges. Liz also loved the lyrics:

The Potter saw a vessel that had been broken by the wind and the rain.

And he sought with so much compassion to put it back together again.

Liz related to those words. They spoke to her. On a subconscious level, she viewed her family as somewhat broken, especially her father. She did everything she could to try and fix him. Later in her life, she would find herself drawn to people, especially men, who seemed to be broken and needed help. She would find herself oversensitive to their needs and formed relationships with men that she thought she could rescue.

* * *

During the testimony portion of the service, all the kids had a way of giving a similar scripted thirty-second testimony.

I give honor to God, to our pastor Bishop Murphy, Mother Murphy, Elder Riley, and his companion. I thank God for being here, thank God for my life, health, and strength. Please pray for me.

This was the standard testimony for all the kids. However, one day Pamela decided to go off script.

"I give honor to God, Bishop Murphy, Mother Murphy, and to Elder and Sister Riley. This song is my testimony," Pamela said. Then she began to sing "I Made a Vow," which was Theresa's signature song. Her voice was more melodic and angelic than Theresa's was. Liz listened intently and was in awe at the four-foot-eleven-inch teenager standing in front of the congregation with the assistance of her crutches. Liz felt a chill travel down her spine and goose bumps rise up on her arms.

Liz watched the expressions on the faces of the adults. Most of them either closed their eyes, nodded their heads, or hummed along. But it was the display of Pam's bravery to stand up and sing and her audacity to sing Theresa's signature song better than Theresa, that most impressed Liz.

After the song ended, the entire church clapped and shouted "Praise God! Hallelujah!"

The lyrics, "I promised him I'll go every step of the way; I made a vow to the Lord," coming from this teenaged disabled girl really struck a chord with the congregation. This monumental moment gave Liz an idea.

"Pam, that was amazing," Liz told Pam after the church service ended.

Pam and Gerlisa were sitting on the back pew of the church.

"Thanks," Pam said blushing. "I've been wanting to sing it for a long time but not in front of Theresa," she continued in a lowered voice.

Liz sat down on the pew in front of them. She didn't notice that Theresa was not in attendance that day. Theresa had begun spending more time at another Seventh-Day church where a young man she fancied had attended. Most of church members had adjourned upstairs to eat. Pamela, Gerlisa, and Liz sat in the back of the church to eat their sandwiches.

"We should sing together," Liz blurted out.

"Yes," Gerlisa quickly agreed.

They already knew the James Cleveland song "Lord, Help Me to Hold Out." Later, Gerlisa taught Liz and Pam a song by Edwin Hawkins called "I Shall Be Free." Their foster mom, Sister Shaw, began dressing Pamela and Gerlisa in matching dresses. Since Pamela didn't want her leg brace to show and pants were not permitted in church, Sister Shaw made sure the dresses were ankle length. Elsie and Liz liked the dresses and thought it would be a good idea for Liz to wear a matching dress too.

Weeks later, when the girls debuted in their matching attire as The Rock of Ages Trio and sang the only two songs that they had in their repertoire, jealousy arose. By this time, Theresa had heard about Pamela singing *her* song and was not happy when her sister confirmed that Pamela sang the song as good as Theresa had and maybe even better. Later, when Bishop Murphy suggested that Pamela, Gerlisa, and Liz join Theresa and Beverly to form a youth choir, the Riley girls balked, especially Theresa, who wanted no competition from Pamela.

"Why do the girls have to sing in separate groups? They should all be singing together," Sister Rossi asked Elsie and Sister Shaw one day after service was over.

Sister Rossi was Beverly's godmother and didn't attend Rock of Ages on a regular basis.

"The Riley girls didn't want to sing with them," Elsie spoke up in the other girls' defense. "So they formed their own group."

Looking flabbergasted, Sister Rossi glanced over at Sister Riley, Theresa and Beverly's mother, for confirmation. Sister Riley closed her eyes as she nodded in the affirmative in Sister Rossi's direction.

The Rock of Ages Trio soon built up a collection of songs and sang at a number of Seventh-Day church programs in the city. Their matching ankle-length dresses were a big hit with the older women in the churches. Pamela began singing "I Made a Vow" at events that Theresa did not attend. Liz began to sing "The Potter" as her testimony song.

One evening, Bishop Murphy, along with a few Rock of Ages members, visited The House of God, a church that Marvin Gaye's father had once pastored and his family had attended years earlier. The current pastor, Elder Sanders, offered Bishop Murphy an opportunity for his church to sing a couple of songs. Bishop Murphy was not expecting this but didn't hesitate to motion for Liz, Pamela, and Gerlisa to represent the church.

Liz's heart raced. They had never performed at this church before. This would be the largest congregation for which they had ever performed. All three girls were nervous, but the trio rose to the occasion and brought down the house. After church that night, Liz felt as if she was floating on a cloud.

"Daddy," she shrieked when she entered the house. Fred was in the bedroom watching television. "We sang two songs at the House of God church tonight. The people loved our singing. You should have heard us."

Liz felt so happy that she thought she would just burst.

"That's nice, Babby," Fred said droopy-eyed and wearing a goofy smile on his face.

Liz knew her father had been drinking.

"You don't understand." She explained, "The House of God church is the home church of Marvin Gaye."

Fred's face showed no indication that he understood what she was talking about.

"You know, Marvin Gaye? Motown? I Heard It Through the Grapevine?"

Fred's fake smile remained plastered in place. She might as well have been sharing her exciting news with her cat Boots. Disappointed, Liz left Fred to his television program.

"Well, goodnight, Daddy," she said in a low tone.

Liz often sought her father's approval when she had done something that excited her. She thought her news would impress him, but he only seemed indifferent to it.

After two years, the Shaw's separated, and Pamela and Gerlisa returned to the foster care system. It was later learned that the Shaw's marriage had supposedly been foreseen by a prophet, at their former church in Virginia, and that they had been told to marry. Unfortunately, the prophet hadn't foreseen that Sister Shaw had already been legally married to someone else, who had been doing time in jail.

This became a sad time for Liz because she treasured her friendship with Pamela and Gerlisa, and singing with them was the only good thing about going to church. It would soon also become a time of disillusionment with the church for Liz, as its distinctive doctrine came in direct opposition with the behavior of some of its members. It would later be discovered that church funds were being misappropriated, and the pastor would father a child with one of the sisters in the church. *So much for, "Thou shalt not steal," and, "Thou shalt not commit adultery,"* Liz thought.

* * *

When Liz was sixteen, she and her mother began attending Mount Zion Assembly, another Seventh-Day church. Liz liked this church, but she felt like a social misfit compared to the other teenage girls.

These girls were allowed to participate in social events like house parties. Liz was invited on a few occasions but always declined. She feared that she would be put in a situation that would make her uncomfortable. She knew these parties involved smoking weed and drinking alcohol. She was not willing to break the rules or suffer any consequences.

She was dubbed a "Goody-Two-shoes" and "stuck-up" because she preferred to hang out with the older women. If they were cleaning the church, Liz would be the only young person there to help. Once the older ladies at the church decided to give Liz a little gift to show their appreciation.

"We would like to present this token of our appreciation to Sister Becky," Sister Patricia announced to the church. "She is the only young person that continuously helps out with the cleaning and the hanging of the curtains."

As the church members applauded, the mother of two other teenage girls spoke up.

"Other girls help out too."

"No other teenager but Becky has ever helped with the cleaning," Mother Magruder, the eldest woman in the church, defended.

"That's right," Sister Sharon echoed. "We're the only two tall enough to hang the curtains."

Liz had mixed feelings about what was taking place. On one hand, she liked being recognized for her good deeds. She thrived on being helpful and being appreciated for her efforts. On the other hand, she knew that she was making the other teenage girls look bad.

When she was seventeen, Liz joined the Mount Zion choir. She loved singing in the choir and prayed that when she died she would become a member in the angelic choir in heaven. All she wanted to do was sing. The church recorded a weekly broadcast that was played on the air every Sunday evening.

"The broadcast is about to come on," Liz shouted, while tuning the radio to the gospel station.

"We will now hear the broadcast from Mount Zion Assembly in Washington, DC," the radio announcer said.

As the choir began to sing, Liz shouted, "That's us."

Fred smiled and listened intently to the entire broadcast. At the end he said, "Very nice."

This was the closest Liz's father would ever get to a church service. She wished that he could have seen and heard her singing with Pamela and Gerlisa. Their trio was on fire, and she longed for him to witness her talents.

Finally the day came when she would get her wish. While preparing for the weekly broadcast, Brother Pace, the choir director, was rehearing with the choir for the broadcast taping that night.

"Okay, we're going to start with "There's a Song in My Heart," he said. "Where's Sister Dinah? She's supposed to lead the song."

"She should be here by now," her younger sister said. "I guess she's running late."

"Well, we don't have another song prepared. I need to know if she's going to make it," Brother Pace said nervously.

"It's okay," Liz chimed in. "I can sing it."

Brother Pace looked skeptical. Liz had only been a background singer up to this point. But if Dinah didn't make it in time, he had to have a backup plan.

"Okay," he said reluctantly. "Let's see what you've got."

Brother Pace played the introduction of the song on the organ and then nodded at Liz when it was time for her to start. She stepped in front of the microphone and began to sing.

There's a song in my heart;

That the world cannot sing;

There is music no mortal can play.

God has banished my fears;

He has dried all of my tears, and

He has taken all my heartaches all away.

As she sang, Liz could feel a chill move over her. She wasn't sure if it was just cold in the church or if it was the Holy Spirit. She knew she had nailed the song but waited intently for Brother Pace to confirm it. When Brother Pace stopped playing, his head was still looking down at the keyboard. When he finally raised his head, a broad smile was plastered across his face.

"Becky, you just made your debut," he said.

Liz was elated. "Yes," Liz shouted in her head.

When Dinah arrived in time for the taping, Brother Pace decided that both Dinah and Liz would sing the song. Liz would sing the verse first, and when it repeated, Dinah would sing. From that day forward, the song had two soloists.

Liz could hardly wait for seven o'clock on Sunday night when the broadcast would air. She told Fred about her solo on the radio, and he was anxious to hear. After the song was finished, he congratulated her.

"Very good, Babby," he said. "I'm proud of you."

Liz felt joy in her spirit. She liked making her father proud. But in her efforts to be a good daughter, she felt that she was missing out on life.

By the time she was twenty-one, she believed herself to be ill prepared to handle a relationship with a man. She had had only one short-lived romance with a teenage boy from her neighborhood and had been on only one movie date with another boy named Victor from high school. She had only brought Victor around to the house a couple of times. After Fred had finished grilling the boy, Liz had been too embarrassed to have any other guys come meet her parents. This would set the stage for some of Liz's most unlikely pairings with men in the future.

Chapter 11

WASHINGTON, DC

2015

"I don't know what my father's upbringing has to do with how I turned out," Liz told her coworker Nicole, who was also a mediator, after being given an assignment by her writing coach. She had been tasked with writing about her father's upbringing and how it had ultimately affected her life.

"I haven't been affected at all," Liz snorted. "I had a wonderful childhood, and he was a good father. I just hated that he drank all the time," Liz said.

"Did you hear what you just said?" Nicole asked in calm voice. "You don't think your father's drinking had any effect on you?"

"I don't see how," Liz replied. "A lot of people had drunk parents, and they lived through it, and so did I. But I'm going to Google it and see what comes up."

Nicole threw Liz a furtive glance. "What exactly are you looking up?" she asked.

"Adult children of alcoholics," Liz replied while typing.

Just tapping her fingers on the keys gave Liz a weird sensation.

Now well past fifty years old, was she actually identifying her father as an alcoholic?

"Huh," Liz said to Nicole as if verbalizing her thoughts might make them digest better. "I never really referred to my father as an alcoholic before, but that's essentially what he was." Liz slipped out a nervous chuckle. "I always said he drank a lot, like that's different."

"So what is your search coming up with?" Nicole asked. "Did you find anything?"

"Well, let's see." Liz scrunched her eyes and leaned closer to her computer screen. "I've got an article here that says, 'The characteristics and personality traits of adult children of alcoholics are fear of losing control,' which I believe is true about me. I am a bit of a control freak, and I hate when things don't go as planned."

"Okay, what else?"

"'They avoid conflict,'" Liz continued, "which I also know is true of me. It says here that 'Adult children of alcoholics have a fear of people in authority and people who are angry, and they do not take personal criticism very well. They have a high burden of responsibility and constantly seek approval.'"

"So how did your parents get along?" Nicole readjusted the topic of conversation. Liz went with the flow.

"Well, by the time I was ten, my brothers had left home and joined the army. Most of the time, my parents didn't speak to each other and used me as their messenger pigeon," Liz said and laughed.

"What do you mean?" Nicole asked. She wasn't laughing with Liz.

"Say for instance, when my mother prepared dinner, she would call me into the kitchen and tell me to go ask my father, who might be upstairs, if he wanted something to eat. So I'd go upstairs and ask, 'Daddy, do you want something to eat?' He would say, 'Yes,' and I'd go back downstairs and tell my mother. So she would fix a plate, and I would carry it up to him."

"So that seemed normal to you?" Nicole asked.

"Yep. We did that quite often."

Nicole watched Liz and kept questioning her. "So, what else is on the list?

"Okay." Liz read from the screen and pushed back feelings of intrusiveness from Nicole. "It's says 'these adult children are weighed down by low self-esteem.'" Liz flinched. "Huh. I don't know about that," she mumbled. "'They adopt compulsive behavior.'" Liz paused. "Well I wouldn't say compulsive but maybe additive."

"What do you mean?" asked Nicole.

"Like, I can go overboard eating certain things like potato chips, especially when I'm stressed."

Nicole nodded knowingly. "I see. Anything else on the list?"

"It says that 'Adult children of alcoholics will do anything to save a relationship rather than face the pain of abandonment, even if the relationship is unhealthy.' That 'they sometimes like to be the *rescuer* and will form relationships with others who need their help, to the extent of neglecting their own needs.'" Liz looked up at Nicole and paraphrased. "What happens is that they place the focus on the needs of someone else so they won't have to focus on their own difficulties and shortcomings.

And," Liz looked back at the screen, 'They tend to marry an alcoholic.'" Liz paused for a moment. Familiarity hit her in the chest like a closely flung brick. She said nothing about this feeling to Nicole.

She continued reading. "'Often they will acquire the characteristics of alcoholics, even if they never drink themselves. They can be in denial, develop poor coping strategies, have an inability to problem solve, and form dysfunctional relationships.'"

Liz felt a bit of a reprieve. "Well, at least my family wasn't dysfunctional," she said.

"Excuse me. What did you just say?" Nicole asked craning her neck forward. "Didn't you just say that when your parents weren't speaking, they used you as their messenger pigeon?"

"Yes," Liz responded and laughed. But the humor felt forced.

Liz realized in that brief moment that she often laughed at or made jokes about serious matters. It seemed to be her go-to coping mechanism when she didn't want to face anything unpleasant or embarrassing. Now the action stood out as surely as red would against white.

"And you don't think that was dysfunctional?" Nicole continued.

"No, like I said, that happened a lot, so it was normal to me."

"Liz, that was dysfunctional," Nicole said in a stern voice.

"Damn! I have a dysfunctional family and don't even know it," Liz joked.

She noticed again that her propensity to joke and make light of difficult situations was clinically termed "avoidance." Liz practiced avoidance a lot. And until today she thought her use of avoidance had served her well. But now, she began to believe that she used avoidance as a crutch.

Nicole looked at her watch and noticed that it was almost nine o'clock.

"Oh, I'm going to have to cut this short. I have a nine o'clock meeting with my boss," she said.

"Okay, we'll talk later," Liz said, looking at Nicole, who was now standing in the doorway.

"Do you want your door opened or closed?" Nicole asked.

"Closed, please."

"Okay, talk to you later."

"Okay, later."

After Nicole left, Liz wondered what other things she had been in denial about. It dawned on her that she was prone to stuffing her feelings deep down inside to the point that she had lost the ability to feel or to express them in most situations. Her husband had once said that Liz seemed indifferent, at times, like she didn't care about things one way or another.

Could he be right? Liz now thought to herself. The article had stated this as a characteristic as well. She thought, *whoa, this article has me pegged to a tee.*

Gazing at the computer monitor, Liz reared back in her chair, clasped her hands behind her head, and tried to recall episodes from her youth. She found that she could remember the incidents but not necessarily the emotions involved.

The part of the article that gave Liz pause was that adult children of alcoholics had a tendency to marry alcoholics. This reminded Liz of the adage that women tended to be attracted to men with similar attributes as their fathers.

Could that be true? She thought. Liz began to examine her past relationships with men.

Chapter 12

SOUTHEAST, WASHINGTON, DC

1976

In the summer of 1976, when Liz was fourteen, the first boy she really liked was her neighbor named CJ. He was a brawny teenager, raging with a bit of scruff and buff and a lot of sexy. He was a rugged boy—the kind you would want to be alone in the wilderness with, for more than one reason. Aside from good looks, CJ was smart, and that was a characteristic even her father had to admire.

Fred had run all the neighborhood boys away, who had showed any interest in his daughter. He was intimidating, and most of the boys hurried past their house when Mr. Smith came outside—all except CJ. CJ came by every day on his bike and stopped to talk to Liz, who was usually on the front porch. Fred's intimidating looks and gruff speech didn't faze CJ in the least. But CJ was always respectful.

One evening Fred decided to invite him to sit on the porch with him and Liz, since it was apparent CJ was determined to converse with Liz even if it meant doing so from the other side of the front gate. This particular evening, Fred decided to get into the conversation by engaging Liz and CJ in a game of naming the

United States' capitols. It became apparent, early in the game, that Fred had met his match.

"What's the capitol of Vermont?" Fred asked.

"Montpelier," CJ replied with confidence.

"Okay, what about North Dakota," Fred asked, trying to stump CJ with ones he thought were hard.

"Bismarck," CJ answered.

Liz didn't even know some of the state capitols CJ recalled with such ease. This made Liz like him even more. He had actually impressed her father.

One day Liz was locked out of the house. She had been visiting with a neighbor across the street. When she returned home, she noticed that her father's car was gone. He didn't know she didn't have her key with her.

Another liquor store run, Liz figured.

But after waiting for an hour on the front porch, Liz was ready to go inside. She went to the back door to check to see if the storm door was unlocked. When she pulled on the door latch, she was pleasantly surprised that the storm door opened. She knew that a spare back door key hung on a nail at the top of the doorframe. The door contained six individual windowpanes. Liz figured if she broke the upper left-hand pane, she could reach the key that hung at the top of the inside doorframe.

She looked around the backyard for something she could use to break the windowpane. Their yard used to be filled with gravel rocks, which served as a rugged surface for a driveway. But her mother wanted grass and flowers, so they gave the gravel rocks to Mona's parents for their driveway. Liz recalled the day when Mona's brothers had come to the house and had filled two red Radio Flyer wagons with the rocks, making several trips until all the rocks had been removed.

Liz finally found a smooth, round rock, which she thought was dense enough to crack the windowpane. Back at the rear door, Liz tapped the pane until it split horizontally. She was able to push the bottom half inside. After she heard the glass hit the kitchen floor and break, something told her to do the same to the top half of the pane. However, she ignored her intuition. Liz put her long, thin arm through the opening and felt along the doorframe for the spare key. When she couldn't locate it, she pulled her arm back out, scraping her bicep on the top half of the glass pane.

"Shit," she cried aloud as she noticed the blood rising from the thin layer of skin that had been sliced by the broken pane.

She placed her other hand over the scrape and began walking toward the front of the house. She didn't have a clue about what she would do next. Then she saw him. It was CJ riding down the sidewalk on his bike.

"Hey," CJ said stopping at her fence, wearing a broad smile on his face.

Liz approached the fence holding her arm with a terrified look in her eyes. CJ's countenance changed to concern.

"What's the matter?"

"I cut my arm trying to break into the house."

"Let me see." Liz held her arm over the fence and lifted her hand just enough for CJ to see the cut.

"Hold on. I'll be right back," he said, spinning his bike around in the opposite direction.

He sped off and went back to his house, which was about six doors down. When he returned, he had first aid antiseptic cream, alcohol pads, cotton balls, sterile gauze, and adhesive tape. Liz looked on with admiration as CJ intently focused on taking care of her wound.

He really cares about me, she thought.

Liz sat on the porch for another forty minutes waiting for Fred to come home and open the door, but now she had CJ with her to keep her company.

"Hi, Mr. Smith," CJ said greeting the returning Fred after he had exited his vehicle.

"Hey, Daddy," Liz said as Fred entered the front gate. "I had a little accident," she continued.

"What happened?" Fred asked in an octave higher than his regular tone of voice and with a clear look of concern on his face.

"I was locked out the house all this time," Liz said.

"Aw, Babby, I'm sorry. I thought you had your key."

"No, I didn't. I tried to get in using the spare key in the kitchen. I broke the windowpane but cut my arm." Fred now focused on the bandage around her arm. "CJ rushed home and brought alcohol and bandages for me. He really helped me out."

Impressed, Fred extended his hand to CJ, and the two engaged in a firm handshake, which seemed to last for several seconds.

"I really appreciate you taking care of my girl," Fred said to CJ, who was smiling. After that, it was official—Liz and CJ were girlfriend and boyfriend.

* * *

"Meet me in the garage in the morning at seven," Liz whispered to CJ on the phone.

The summer mornings offered the straight-laced, non-rule-breaking Liz a rare opportunity to spend time alone with CJ. Her mother had to be at work at seven in the morning, so she was out of the house at six. Her father worked the midnight shift and didn't get off until eight in the morning.

"Okay, but be sure you unlock the back gate," CJ replied.

"I will," Liz said.

Her voice cracked. Her stomach quivered with a mix of excitement and nervousness. Liz took the padlock and chain off the gate of their six-foot high fence. Fred had had the high fence installed to deter people from hopping the back fence and cutting through their yard.

When she heard the neighborhood dogs barking from three doors away, she knew that CJ was coming down the alley. She ran into the garage and hid. Her heart pounded when she heard the back gate open and then clap shut. The door opened slowly, allowing light to stream into the dark, windowless building. CJ entered and walked past her, not seeing her as she crouched down. She contained her urge to giggle but only for a moment. She leaped out from her hiding place and jumped on CJ's back.

"Whoa," he said laughing while grabbing onto her legs and hoisting her up onto his back. He spun her around, and she held him tight around his neck. She felt uninhibited, and it was a wonderful feeling, but then the feeling left her almost as quickly as it had come over her.

"Put me down. You're making me dizzy," she squealed.

CJ promptly did as he was asked. He turned to face her. He held her in his strong arms and looked deep into her eyes. This level of intimacy made Liz uncomfortable, but she loved looking into his hazel-brown eyes. His eyes were like none she'd ever seen before. But she feared what he might see looking into her eyes. Could he see the true Liz if he looked deep enough? Would he be able to tell that she was riddled with self-doubt? That she felt like an oddball—a social misfit? His soft lips enveloped hers, and her fears evaporated.

Liz and CJ's morning rendezvous continued through the end of the summer. She had thought about moving their meeting place from the garage to her bedroom many times. She was sure they wouldn't be caught, but there was always that nagging feeling that just when she decided to be daring, Fred would come home early. It helped that CJ never pressured her about sex. He was a perfect gentleman. Sometimes she thought he was too perfect. He seemed to really like her, or dare she think, maybe even love her? He might have felt for her what she had always dreamed someone would—like in those loves songs she listened to on the stereo. CJ could be her dream come true.

* * *

Liz rang in the new year of 1977 listening to Casey Kasem's top one hundred songs of 1976. She couldn't believe Paul McCartney and Wings' "Silly Love Songs" was number one. She saw CJ early on New Year's Day.

"Hey, I have something for you," CJ said stopping his bike at her front gate.

"For me?" Liz questioned, taking the gold-tone ring that CJ presented to her.

"Yeah. Since y'all don't celebrate Christmas, I thought I'd wait until now to give you the gift I bought you."

Liz gazed at the ring. It was unusual. She had never seen one like it. It was a heart held, on each side, by hands, and the heart had a crown on top of it.

"It's a Claddagh ring," CJ said. "It represents love, loyalty, and friendship," he explained, slipping the ring on her left ring finger.

"Thank you," Liz whispered.

Staring at the thoughtful gift, Liz wondered if she was worthy of such adoration. She worried that she couldn't reciprocate in kind.

Over the next few months, Liz found herself pulling away from CJ. It started with a call from his older sister, Carla.

"Hello," Liz said answering the telephone.

"Hi, this is Carla," the voice said on the other end of the line.

"Oh, hi," Liz said curiously.

"We're having a party Saturday night, and I'm calling to invite you."

Liz's heart skipped a beat. Her stomach quivered. She felt a lump rise up in her throat, and she thought she might choke. After what seemed like a long pause, Liz swallowed hard.

"Er, I don't think I can make it on Saturday," Liz lied. "But thanks for asking."

"Oh, okay," Carla said, her response sounding questioning.

After they ended the call, Liz lay face down on her bed. "You Should Be Dancing" by The Bee Gees was playing on the radio. Her mind raced. She felt like a square peg that didn't fit into the round world. She couldn't relate to the world outside the confines of her home. She didn't dance. She was a church girl, who was restricted from participating in all things worldly.

She constantly felt embarrassed by her home life. She felt uncool at school. She didn't like being different but didn't know how to change. She didn't have the courage to stand up for herself against her parents' restrictive rules. She resented the fact that her brothers were able to negotiate their way out of going to church and seemed to get away with their rebellious ways. But she couldn't. She was the good child, and the weight of carrying this label felt like an inescapable burden.

* * *

That May, John and his wife Celeste, along with her son Tony, were visiting the house. An argument broke out between Elsie and Celeste. Little Tony had been misbehaving. Elsie had corrected him, and Celeste hadn't liked it. After heated words were exchanged, Celeste stormed out the house. John took his wife's side and left the house too. More severe words were still flying back and forth between Elsie and Celeste as Celeste and John exited the front gate. Fred stayed out of it, not saying a word, as did Liz. But John felt he had to speak up and defend his wife.

As Celeste, John, and little Tony crossed the street to their car, John turned, pointed his finger at his family, who were all standing on the front porch, and said, "All you motherfuckers can go to hell."

In that moment for Liz, the world stood still.

What did I do to be included in that hateful statement? So now

I'm a motherfucker that can go to hell for all you care, big brother? Liz screamed in her head.

Liz went inside the house and stood at the front door while her parents remained on the porch. Several neighbors were outside on their porches, in their yards, or on the street. They witnessed the whole thing, including CJ, who was on his bike. This infuriated Liz.

Now the entire neighborhood knows how fucked up this family is, she thought. "No John, you go to hell," Liz mumbled.

She turned on her heels, raced up the stairs to her room, and slammed the door. She buried her face in her pillow and beat the mattress. "I hate it. I hate it," she screamed into the pillow.

She felt all the anxiety, fear, shame, and anger, which she had stuffed down, spill out of her. It was like a dam broke, and all it took was her brother telling her and her parents to go to hell. She felt so betrayed by him.

The following day, Liz sat on her front stoop still seething over John and Celeste's behavior the day before. She felt that John had changed when he married Celeste. He went against the family now, and that was all due to her influence. It was like he broke the secret code that you don't air the family's dirty laundry.

"How ya doing?" CJ asked, breaking into Liz's thoughts. She had not seen or heard him when he rode up on his bike.

"Hey," she said holding her right hand over her eyes, shielding them from the sun's glare.

"So what was that with your brother?" CJ asked.

Liz stiffened. She didn't want to discuss it with him. She was embarrassed. Her eyes were fixed and she stared past CJ.

"There was a misunderstanding," she finally said after a long pause.

"I'll say it was. Out here cussing your parents out," CJ said.

Liz blinked and she felt a shift in her spirit. *Is he judging us? Who does he think he is?*

Her reaction to his comment seemed like a perfect time to lash out at him.

"You don't know anything about my family," she screamed.

She was on her feet now and standing directly in front of him. Only the fence stood between them. Suddenly, everything around her appeared out of focus. She couldn't even make out the string of expletives that spilled out of her mouth at CJ. When things came back into focus, she could see both hurt and anger on CJ's face. He said something, but her intense emotional state did not allow her ears to hear him.

He then spun his bike around in the opposite direction and began to ride away. In that moment, an emotional Liz twisted the ring he'd given her off her finger and flung it at him. The ring flew past him and onto the ground. She quickly spun around and ran in the house. She never spoke to CJ again.

Chapter 13

WASHINGTON, DC

2015

On the train ride home after work, Liz recalled her high school years as being, for the most part, uneventful. By the eleventh grade, she had not had a steady boyfriend since CJ, and no one at the school interested her until one day in mid-November 1978, a new student was assigned to her Journalism class. He was a transfer student from California named Charles Hawkins.

Whoa! Who is he? Liz asked herself. *He looks like a grown ass man.*

At sixteen, Charles had a full beard and mustache. He looked very mature. Liz did not even know she could find a bearded man so attractive. She was sure that he must be at least eighteen, but he wasn't. She later learned that he was actually three months younger than she was.

They got to know each other during the teacher's strike at Ballou High School in March of 1979. He told her that his father was a master sergeant in the air force, that he had a younger brother, and that his family lived in military housing on Bolling Air Force Base. But Charles and Liz would have a falling out over a ring.

"That's a nice ring," Charles said one day while he and Liz were walking to a 7-Eleven store near the school. He was referring to a gold ring Liz wore with the initial "E" inscribed on it.

"Thanks. It's my mother's," Liz replied.

"Oh, okay then. I won't ask you for it," Charles said.

"You can wear it," Liz said gleefully twisting the ring off and handing it to him. When it was apparent that his fingers were too big to fit the ring, Liz ignored her instincts to take the ring back. Things were going so well with Charles, and she didn't want to displease him.

"Just get a chain and wear it around your neck," she suggested. Days later, Charles called, having to admit that her ring was destroyed.

"What happened?" Liz shouted into the phone.

"I put the ring on my pinky finger and couldn't get it off. It was cutting off the circulation in that finger. My father had to take me to the emergency room. They had to cut the ring off my finger."

"You cut my ring?" Liz screamed. Her head felt as though it was going to explode and hit the ceiling. "Didn't I tell you to put the ring on a chain and wear it around your neck?"

"It was either cut the ring or cut off my finger," Charles responded somewhat sarcastically. He couldn't believe how insensitive Liz was being.

Frankly, I would have preferred they cut off your goddamn finger, Liz thought. "Just bring the ring to school tomorrow," Liz finally said.

She slammed down the receiver. The following day, Liz was furious when she saw the ring. The medics had cut the ring in two places in order to remove it safely from Charles's pinky finger. She looked in horror at the pieces of gold that were once her ring. She wanted to kill Charles.

"I'm sorry," Charles said.

Yes, you are a sorry little shit, Liz thought.

She turned and walked away from him without responding.

They didn't see each other or speak again for more than two years after that incident.

Liz's senior year of high school was unexciting. Charles had dropped out of school during their senior year, and there were no other boys that she was interested in. She didn't attend her prom because no one asked. It was just as well, she would have most likely declined. Her Holy Roller church upbringing forbade dancing and parties, so she never really learned to dance and felt self-conscious about her ability.

Once while babysitting her two-year-old nephew, Tony, she had playfully held the boy in her arms and had danced around the porch.

CJ had been at the fence on his bike and had commented, "You can't dance."

Liz had immediately stopped. His comment had bothered her because she had hated to be criticized or mocked.

* * *

In her twenties and early thirties, Liz went through a phase where she was in relationships with older men. She felt that she was ready to settle down, to get married, and to start a family. However, men who were her own age were noncommittal.

She met Doug in 1984, when she was twenty-two. She and her mother moved into the town house next door to him a few months after Fred had died. Doug was fourteen years older, was separated, but was still legally married to his second wife. He had four children by three different mothers. And like her father, Doug was a drinker and a smoker.

Four months after moving next door to Doug, Liz got her own apartment in a high-rise apartment building, and they began dating. But after dating for almost a year, Doug attempted to end the relationship with Liz.

"You are a young, smart, and beautiful women," Doug said one night sitting at the dining room table in Liz's fifth-floor apartment. "You will find someone else, and it won't take you that long," he said, placing her door key on the table. They weren't living together but she gave him a key to show her level of commitment to the relationship.

Liz sat motionless as tears welled up in her eyes. She always wanted to be wanted and needed. She did everything to please. She didn't understand why he was trying to end the relationship. He was essentially telling her that he was not good enough for her and could not give her what she wanted. But Liz could not except that reasoning. She took his wanting to end things with her as a rejection of her and that she had failed to be what he had wanted in a woman.

"No," she said as a single teardrop rolled down her cheek. She needed the relationship to work. Failure was not an option. She couldn't be the woman who was unable to hold onto a man. She'd do anything to save the relationship.

After two years, Liz moved into Doug's place. By this time, her mother had sold her townhouse next door and had moved into another house about five miles away. Relocating to Doug's benefited him more than it did Liz. He began to have financial hardship after his wife filed for child support and divorce.

It soon became apparent to Liz that her idea of their living arrangement differed from his. He immediately took issue with her displaying her family pictures in the living room. He referenced the picture she had taken with her three young nieces: Yavonne, who was nine; Regina, who was five; and Rachel, who was one. In the photograph, Liz and the girls were all dressed in yellow and white.

"I don't want my friends coming in here asking me about these pictures," Doug argued one day after having had a few beers. "My friends will be saying stuff like, 'I didn't know your old lady had three kids.'"

"What is your problem," Liz asked, annoyed by the frivolous

complaint. "Who the hell gives a rat's black ass what your friends think? And if I did have three kids, so what? You got four kids and three baby mamas."

Doug resented when Liz *talked back* like this. He looked down at his hands as if he was trying to will them to stay in control and not to strike. But six months after moving in, Doug could no longer control his hands. One Thursday night, Doug slapped Liz square in the mouth with an open left hand during an argument. Liz cupped her hand over her mouth and gave Doug a tearful gaze for several seconds. When he reached out to embrace her, she knocked his outreached arms away and ran upstairs to the spare bedroom where she cried herself to sleep. She slept there the rest of the night.

The next morning she looked at her face in the bathroom mirror. Her bottom lip was bruised and swollen. Anger ignited in the pit of her stomach.

I don't have to take this shit from no damn body, she thought. *My father never laid a hand on me, and I'll be damned if this motherfucker is going to start.*

She exited the bathroom and went downstairs to use the kitchen phone.

"Hey, Mary, this is Liz," she said speaking to her employer. "Listen, I fell down the stairs and twisted my ankle. I'd like to take sick leave today," Liz said, lying to her boss while retrieving some ice from the freezer. When she ended her call, she turned to find Doug standing behind her looking remorseful.

"Listen." He began to speak, but Liz raised her right hand up to stop him.

"Save it," she said. "There is nothing you can say to me right now that I will believe. You know my father didn't hit me, and I'm not about to let you or anyone else start hitting me. I'm not one of your children," she said pushing past him. "Got me having to call my boss and lying about why I can't come to work over this bullshit," she mumbled aloud, walking toward the stairs. When she reached the bottom step, she whipped around and locked eyes with Doug. He was standing with his hands folded at his crotch. After a few seconds, he cast down his eyes in an attempt to look submissive.

"And if I tell my brothers that you hit me, they will come over here and kill your monkey ass."

Doug lifted his head and looked at Liz with wide eyes. The glimpse of fear that Liz saw in his eyes gave her great satisfaction.

For the next three weeks, Liz contrived to make her exit from Doug's residence. He worked the evening shift as a computer operator and generally left for work at four-thirty in the evening. Liz avoided seeing him by arriving back at the house after she was sure he was gone. She applied for an apartment in southeast DC and was accepted for immediate occupancy. She told Doug she would be leaving at the end of the month although she had taken possession of the apartment a week before the month ended. This gave her time to move her personal belongings out while he was at work. The rest of her furniture was in storage.

The day had finally come when she would move out of Doug's town house and be gone for good.

"You got one of my albums," Doug announced after looking in the album cabinet of the entertainment center the day of Liz's move.

"What album?" Liz asked. Her reply was curt.

"The Whispers," he said.

Liz didn't let her nervousness show as she confidently walked over to the entertainment center and flipped through the collection of albums until she found The Whispers' "Just Gets Better with Time" album. She knew it was one of his favorite albums, so the night before the move while Doug had been at work, Liz had taken a kitchen knife and had scratched the album on both sides.

"Here it is," she said, pulling the album out to show him.

"Oh," he said looking dumbfounded. Liz quickly placed the album back where she had found it, happy that he didn't inspect it closer and discover the damage she had caused. She gathered the last of her personal items and placed the front door key on the glass dining room table. As she headed for the door, she stopped. She turned and glared at him.

"Let me tell you one thing," Liz said. "You don't have anything in this house that I couldn't get on my own if I wanted it. I don't have to steal from the likes of you." She left his house and didn't look back.

In her new apartment, Liz waited for her new sofa and full-sized bed to be delivered. She felt proud of herself that she was able to break free from what was obviously a bad situation. Yet the feeling of disappointment overshadowed her. She had made a poor choice with Doug. She felt that the years she had spent with him had been a colossal waste of her time and youth. Now at the age of twenty-five, she was looking for a new love. And as Doug had predicted, it wouldn't take that long.

Chapter 14

WASHINGTON, DC

1987

Liz met Sam when she transferred to the federal agency where he also worked. She was hired as a human resources assistant, and he was a realty officer. His job was to resell agency properties that had been repossessed due to default on home loans.

Sam was striking. He was tall and slim with rich caramel-colored skin, thick, curly jet-black hair, and piercing hazelnut-brown eyes. Sam was thirteen years older than Liz, which she didn't consider a drawback.

In the *getting to know you* phase of their relationship, Sam treated Liz to lunch at Popeye's.

"So, do you smoke?" Liz asked after they sat down with their food.

"I smoke cigars," Sam replied.

Liz hated the smell of cigars more than cigarettes. This should have been a deterrent. She really didn't want to accept another smoker in her life. Her father had died from emphysema as a result of cigarette smoking. Yet, she didn't feel that she should judge him based on this vice.

"Do you drink?" She asked.

"Like a fish," he replied.

"Oh, boy," Liz said joking. *He smokes stinky cigars and drinks like a fish,* she thought. "Great," she said sarcastically under her breath. Liz wondered why she always seemed to be attracted to men who were drinkers and smokers and also seemed to be emotionally unavailable. Why couldn't she make herself be attracted to Gary, the nice guy in the mail room, who bought her cute stuffed animals and flowers?

"Why do women always want the guys that treat them badly?" Gary had once asked Liz.

He seriously wanted to know what was wrong with him. At the time, she honestly did not know the answer. But in later years, Liz realized that on some level she didn't really believe she deserved a nice guy. Like with CJ, she had purposely destroyed her relationship with him all those years ago for the same reason.

Sam was attracted to Liz but had limited time to spend with her. But more importantly, he was unwilling to make more time in his life for her. He was devoted to his duties as a Freemason, and his obligations as a past grand master kept him at lodge meetings and events on a regular basis.

Liz eventually grew tired of Sam's devotion to the lodge and its members. She tried to exercise patience and understanding in the hope that these qualities would endear her to him. But Sam's commitment to the Freemasons and noncommitment to her finally wore thin. After three years, she decided to move on, and they parted as friends.

1995

By the time Liz was thirty-three years old, she was resigned to the fact that she would never marry or have children of her own. For the past five years, she had devoted much of her time to the church services her mother had begun presiding over in her home. Members consisted of three families—a total of seven adults and six children. Five of the children were Liz's nieces and nephew. They still observed the Seventh-Day Sabbath but did not adhere to the strict dress code.

One day, Liz met a man at work named Ray. He was an older gentleman, seventeen years her senior. Somewhere in their conversation, she expressed a desired to have some work done at her house. She was now living in the house her mother had bought after she had sold the town house next door to Doug.

"I have a very old little house," she told him. "I have wood-paneled walls and acoustical drop-ceiling tiles."

"I know how to put in drywall," Ray offered. "I can do it for you and not charge an arm and leg."

Liz decided to hire Ray and was excited to have her little house modernized a bit. Almost immediately, Ray expressed an attraction and interest in Liz although she did not reciprocate the feelings at first. She wasn't at all physically attracted to him but didn't consider herself to be so shallow that she would not give someone a chance, even if they didn't fit her physical type.

He had been married twice and had three children. The youngest, a daughter, was ten. He told Liz that he was divorced from his second wife but every Friday he was in court settling property matters.

I thought all that kind of stuff was ironed out before the divorce was final, she thought to herself. *Oh well. What do I know?* She surmised.

Not wanting to have a suspicious mind, Liz ignored many alarm bells that rang in her head each time she thought something was off about Ray. Before long, they spoke of moving in together and getting married.

However, she had never visited his home in southeast Washington, DC. He had said that he feared his two large Akita dogs would attack her. He had also said that he didn't want them to live at his house or hers and that he wanted them to have a house of their own with no memories of past partners.

Liz had spent months working with a realtor searching for a house for the two of them, only to have Ray give some excuse why he had not liked it. Time was running out. They would be married in two months after a nearly one-year-long courtship. The date was set for August 9th. Her best friend, Tina, had agreed to be her maid of honor, and her friend Donna from Alabama, was flying up with her daughter to serve as her matron of honor. But two weeks before the wedding date, Ray dropped a bomb.

"Listen. I have to tell you something," Ray said sitting at the kitchen table in Liz's house.

"What is it?" Liz asked, noticing that he was not making eye contact. She sat down in the chair across from him and leaned forward. She studied his face and tried to figure out what could possibly have him looking so serious. Her stomach felt like butterflies were fluttering about inside. She started to feel queasy.

"I had a dream last night that disturbed me," he continued.

Liz sat back in her chair. She craned her neck to the left, heard it crack, and then released a heavy sigh.

"Yeah?" She questioned with a frown forming on her face.

"My mother came to me in my dream and said, 'You're not ready to get married.'"

Liz paused for several seconds. She returned to a forward lean and rested her chin on her hand.

"Really?" Liz asked. She didn't know whether to laugh or to cry. She thought this was beyond preposterous.

"Yes." Ray continued casting his eyes down toward the glass tabletop. "I told my sister about the dream, and she said that she agreed with Mama—that I'm not ready to get married right now."

Liz thought she could actually feel her blood boiling. The sinking, sick feeling in the pit of her stomach now felt like fire, and the temperature got so hot she broke out in a sweat. Liz narrowed her eyes, and when she began to speak, her voice was low and stern.

"You don't have to use your dead mother or your sister to get out of marrying me. That's the weakest shit I've ever heard. Your mother came to you in a dream," Liz mocked. "Give me a fucking break. I know six-year-olds that can lie better than that."

"I'm not lying. It's true."

"Well isn't that just great," Liz said, now standing up. "Well I just want to thank your mother," she said while looking toward the ceiling with her arms stretched upward. "Thank you, Ray's mother." Then Liz bent her body downward with her face parallel to the floor. With outstretched arms, she once again said, "Thank you, Ray's mother, wherever you are."

Fred at Booker T. High School
Norfolk, Virginia

Fred in the U.S. Air Force

George Frink

Reverend Samuel Frink and wife, Louisa

John (top), Liz (middle), Rodney (bottom)

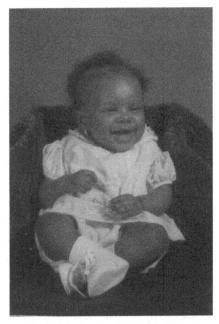

Fred's first grandchild, Kenji

Liz and Yavonne day of Fred's funeral

Elsie and Yavonne, 1983

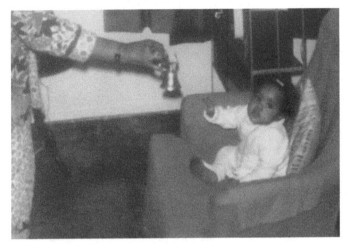

Granddaughter, Regina in Fred's swivel chair and brass bell

Fred and Liz on Bolling Air Force Base, Washington, DC

Chapter 15

CAPITOL HEIGHTS, MD

2015

Liz exited the train, still pondering the conversation she had had with Nicole that morning and how many traits she possessed on that laundry list of adult children of alcoholics. She'd often heard that girls grow up and look for a mate like their father. Had She done that? Was her husband like her father? She didn't think so, but she never really thought about it before.

Driving home, she recalled the week that she had first moved into her home. She had purchased the house 'as is' through the Veterans Administration in 1997. Her old friend Sam had actually helped her secure the bid. One afternoon, she had been sitting in the living room with the insurance man when a blast from her past had called on the telephone.

"Hello," Liz answered.

"Hello, may I speak to Becky," the caller said. Liz had paused and searched her mind about who could have been calling her Becky. It had to be someone from the church or the old neighborhood. But somehow, the deep raspy voice sounded very familiar to her.

"This is she," Liz replied.

"Oh, hi. This is Charles Hawkins."

"Hey, Charles," Liz screamed. "Long time. What you been up to?"

"Nothing much. I got your number from directory assistance. I called you Becky because I wasn't sure the E. M. Smith listed was you."

"Oh yeah. I never list my full name," Liz said. "Hey, I'd like to catch up, but right now I've got to go. I'm here talking with the insurance man. Want to get together this weekend and have lunch?"

"Yes, I'd like that, but can we do that lunch in about two weeks?" Charles asked.

"Sure, it's a date.

The gap between high school and their reconnection had felt seamless. A year later, Charles and Liz were married in a June ceremony at the county courthouse. Afterward, they had gone to a nearby park and fed the ducks, a ritual taken from a page of her own parents' wedding day in Florida, some forty years prior.

Like her father, Charles too had been a drinker and a smoker. These vices would prove to be a source of animosity for Liz. Also like Fred, Charles had not always been reliable. She recalled having returned home from a Chicago trip, and Charles failing to pick her up from the airport on time.

"Hello, this is Liz. My plane will be arriving at Reagan National at 2:00 p.m.," Liz had said, leaving a voice message after the beep. *Where the hell is he?* She thought as she boarded the plane at O'Hare airport.

When she arrived at Reagan National, she called again but had got the answering machine. Somehow she had known he had been home, asleep, and drunk. She was livid.

I knew I should have just driven my car and parked at the airport parking lot. The few dollars I saved getting him to come pick me up is so not worth it, she thought.

"Hey, it's me again. I'm here at the airport at Gate 10," she said as if she were singing. A few minutes later, she had called again and had gotten the answering machine. "Hello, are you there? Where are you? I'm in the baggage claim area now. I got my bag. Just waiting on you," she had said sarcastically.

After an hour, Liz was ready to take public transportation home. But then she had an idea to text message her next-door neighbor.

"Hi. This is Liz. Can you tell me if both cars are in my driveway?"

"Just one car is in the driveway," her neighbor responded.

"Okay, thanks," she texted back. *He must be on his way*, she thought. When she finally found him back at the gate, she was seething.

"Hey, there," Charles said.

All he had to do was add the word Babby, and it would be Fred all over again, she thought.

"Hey," she had said in a flat tone. "Did you get any of my messages? I called you like five times."

"Sorry," he said.

"Yes, I know," she had mumbled.

*   *   *

Thinking back, Liz could only blame herself for her choices in life, whether they were good, bad or indifferent. But the article she and Nicole had read earlier that day finally gave her a glimpse into the root cause of the decisions she made. Her people-pleasing behavior had worked against her. Her tendency to stuff her emotions down in an attempt to avoid conflict had caused her to become passive-aggressive in her marriage. When she was angry with Charles, she could go for long stretches of time without speaking to him.

This is so my parents all over again. She thought.

The article also said that adult children of alcoholics confuse love with pity and tend to love people they can rescue. She recalled that when Charles had reemerged into her life, he had lost his job with the National Cathedral and had been back living with his parents after losing his apartment. He had just started working at Maryland Park and Planning Commission when he called Liz that day. That's why he had needed two weeks before taking her to lunch—he had been waiting on his first paycheck. She had helped him get a position in the government with paid leave and benefits, helped pay off his debts, and rebuild his credit.

Today she learned that adult children of alcoholics either became alcoholics themselves, marry alcoholics, or take on characteristics of alcoholics.

I think it's time for me to face the facts. I have a problem that needs to be dealt with head on, she thought. As she pulled into her driveway, she thought, *my name is Liz Hawkins, and I'm the adult child of an alcoholic.*

Chapter 16

OXON HILL, MARYLAND

1982

Fred's swivel rocker coddled his five-foot eleven-inch frame, which now only carried 130 pounds. Liz called this chair "command central" because Fred ruled the roost from that seat, and everybody knew that *nobody sat in that chair but Fred*. Its soft apricot color belied the lion of a man that had once been her daddy.

He now sat on a donut cushion that helped to alleviate the pain in his coccyx area. Frail from the effects of emphysema, Fred had long given up cigarettes, but his desire for the drink had never left him. His apricot chair wrapped him in comfort and soothed him as he rocked occasionally while watching the evening news on the television. It also partnered with him to harbor stashed bottles of booze—contraband whose very existence excited Fred so much that he'd lose his breath momentarily at the thought of it.

Fred leaned over to the right side of his chair straining to feel for the bottle of gin underneath. The tips of his fingers glided across the floor from front to back, but no liquor bottle was found. The exhaustion winded him, and he sat up straight in the chair as oxygen flowed in his nostrils from his cylinder oxygen tank. He opened his mouth to get air to his lungs faster.

I just need a little taste, he thought.

As his breathing returned to some degree of normalcy, Fred leaned to the left to see if the gin bottle was under the other side of the chair. He ran his left hand down the side of the chair in a slow deliberate motion until the tips of his fingers touched down on the floor. He held onto the arm of the chair with his right hand to steady himself. He reached further under the chair, but the extended position caused his nasal tube to disconnect.

"Shit," Fred said in a whispered voice.

He was panting from the exhaustion and frustrated with the time and energy he had to expend on this one task. His wife, Elsie, was in the bedroom with their granddaughter Yavonne. He dared not ask her to help him find the liquor bottle.

I want a drink not a lecture, he thought.

Fred reconnected the nasal tube to the cannula, which was the device used to deliver the airflow. The feel of the oxygen flowing in his nostrils comforted him. He relied on it. He believed that it was literally his lifeline.

After a few minutes, he went back to the task of locating the liquor bottle. This time he leaned forward, reaching between his legs. Finally, he felt the tip of the bottle. Grasping the arm of the chair with his left hand, Fred leaned forward just a bit further until he could grab the bottle. He grunted at the extra effort, but he was successful.

Too tired to go to the kitchen for a glass of ice, Fred rang his brass bell for help. Yavonne ran into the living room looking eager to grant her grandpa's request.

"Did you ring the bell, Papa?"

"Yes, dear. Will you bring Papa a piece of ice?" Fred asked the four-year-old. Yavonne was quite an astute child but also very literal. She ran into the kitchen and pulled the step stool up to the refrigerator in order to reach the freezer. She plucked one ice cube out the tray, following her papa's instructions to the letter and returned to the living room.

"Here you go, Papa," Yavonne said, proudly plopping the single ice cube into Fred's hand. She then promptly skipped back to the bedroom where she resumed playing with her doll.

I did say to bring me a piece of ice, Fred thought.

He laughed, and his laughter soon turned into a combination of laughing and coughing. Yavonne reminded Fred so much of Liz when she had been a little girl. He loved Yavonne's innocence and youthful exuberance. He loved how animated she could be while telling a story and her peppiness when fulfilling a task. Fred could tell by the look in Yavonne's eyes that she truly believed she had accomplished something great when she retrieved the ice cube for him. He loved Yavonne as much as he loved his own daughter. And to Fred, just like Liz, Yavonne could do no wrong.

He was still holding the melting ice cube when Liz returned home from her afternoon class at Strayer College.

"Hey, what's up?" Liz said when she entered the apartment. When Fred saw Liz, his eyes lit up.

"Hey, Babby, will you bring me a glass?" Fred asked Liz, still chuckling about Yavonne. Liz dropped her book bag on the sofa and headed into the kitchen. When she returned, she handed him an eight-ounce-sized glass.

"So, what's funny?" Liz asked Fred.

"I made the mistake of asking Yavonne to bring me a piece of ice," Fred said, plopping the single cube in the glass.

Liz picked up her book bag and then shot Fred a knowing look.

"Yeah, well she gave you what you asked for," Liz said in a sarcastic tone.

In that moment, Liz realized why Fred wanted a glass of ice.

He probably has a stash on him, Liz thought disapprovingly.

Without saying another word, Liz flung her book bag over her shoulder and promptly went to her room. Fred was all too familiar with his daughter's disapproving look.

When he had no longer been able to drive, Fred had often persuaded Liz to take him to the drive-through window of Strick's Liquor Store on Branch Avenue. She had hated these requests but had never verbally declined them. But her feelings had shown on her face and in her heavy sighs of exasperation.

Liz was torn by her father's drinking. On one hand, church doctrine taught her to honor her father. On the other hand, she didn't want him killing himself or anyone else out there while driving drunk. She imagined him in his car, wrapped around a telephone pole, or veered into oncoming traffic.

She loved him, and she'd hoped that his love for her would be enough to stop him from drinking. But the drink was more important. So she decided if she couldn't stop his drinking, then damn it, she could keep him from being spattered all over Branch Avenue.

Fred cringed under his daughter's knowing look, which signaled to him that she knew he had a stash of liquor tucked somewhere under his chair's citadel. He also knew she didn't know how he got it.

Fred's doctor had just told him to stop drinking immediately and that alcohol decreased lung function. Since Liz and Elsie wouldn't get his liquor for him, Fred devised a new plan.

Desperate times call for desperate measures, he thought.

His ace in the hole proved to be his favorite daughter-in-law, Joanette.

"Next time you come by, will you bring me a pint of gin?" Fred asked Joanette one day when it was just the two of them in the room.

"Okay, Daddy," Joanette said, agreeing to his request with as much exuberance as little Yavonne had. He liked that about Joanette. She was very agreeable. Liz used to be that way, but as she got older, Fred noticed that his daughter had become more cynical. Still, the dutiful daughter, Liz, helped her parents with grocery shopping, writing out the bills, and whatever else was needed, but she appeared to be simply going through the motions. There was once a time when Fred had asked Liz to do something for him or bring him something, he couldn't remember what, but she had balked.

"Augh," she had uttered under her breath. "There's no rest for the weary."

This had hurt Fred. He had already felt that he was a burden on his family. Now his daughter's apparent annoyance had confirmed this belief.

"It's okay. I won't be here much longer," Fred had said in a solemn tone.

"Oh, my God," Liz said grimacing.

She had ended up getting or doing whatever it was that he had asked, but the exchange between them had left him feeling distraught.

Fred reached for his hidden stash of gin or "white lightening in a bottle" as he sometimes called it. He held the pint-sized bottle in his left hand and stared at it for several seconds. He relied on it to soothe him and take his mind away from the fact that he was not always there for his family. Although he was there physically, he was ill equipped to be the strong father figure that his children deserved.

Fred unscrewed the cap of the bottle. He closed his eyes and took a whiff of the gin. It always smelled like pine trees to him. He looked around to make sure the coast was clear and then picked up the glass and slowly poured gin into it until it was full. The first sip felt warm gliding down his throat. It felt so good he squeezed his eyes shut and his body shook.

"Ah, that's good."

Fred screwed the cap back onto the bottle. As quick as possible, he returned his liquid salvation back to its hiding place under the apricot chair—command central—his comrade and keeper of secrets. Fred felt all right. He finished his drink and snuggled down into the tranquility of his chair. Wrapped in its arms, he gently rocked himself to sleep.

* * *

Fred was startled awake when he felt the empty glass slip from his hand. He had been dreaming that the glass had been falling to the floor. He flinched. When he opened his eyes he saw that it was Elsie who had taken the glass from him.

"Do you want something to eat?" Elsie asked, looking over her shoulder at Fred but still walking toward the kitchen.

"Whatcha got cooking?" he asked.

"There's some leftover liver and onions I can heat up," Elsie called out from the kitchen.

"No, I don't think I want that," Fred said, feeling a knot forming in the pit of his stomach. "I don't have much of an appetite these days."

"I guess not," Elsie said sarcastically, now standing in the living room with Fred. "You know liquor kills the appetite."

Fred knew he had been caught because Elsie had retrieved the glass from him while he had napped. He didn't respond. He just gave her a little smirk.

"Well, you need to eat something," Elsie continued. "How about an Ensure shake?"

"What flavor do we have?"

"We have chocolate, vanilla, and eggnog flavors."

"I might have one a little later," Fred said, deciding that his stomach felt too unsettled at the moment.

"Okay." Elsie returned to the kitchen to get something to eat for herself.

Fred listened with great intensity at the rustling of pots and pans in the kitchen. He heard the rhythm and blues music coming from the stereo in Liz's room. He listened to Yavonne, who was sitting in the hallway outside Liz's bedroom door talking to her baby doll.

Yavonne always wants to be in Becky's room, but Becky rarely let's her in, Fred thought. *Sitting outside the door is as close as she's going to get.*

It pained Fred to see Yavonne on the outside of a place he knew she craved to be inside of. Fred was all too familiar with being just outside the reach of one's desire. Look but don't touch. Wasn't that the reality of life?

Even as a child, Fred had eaten dinner each night with a neighbor family whose head had been his very own father. Yet no one had told him who the man had really been. Fred had so admired the family and had really enjoyed his time spent with them. "Look at the beautiful family that you're allowed to eat with and visit with," life seemed to be telling him. "But the reality is that you cannot ever be a part of this family or touch your God-given lineage because you're illegitimate ... on the outside." Fred identified with Yavonne's longing.

Nostalgic and pensive, he scanned the parameter of the living room, focusing on every piece of furniture. Above the golden slipcovered sofa hung an oil painting of a lake with a sycamore tree planted beside the water. The gold and orange leaves fell from its branches. The matching marble-topped end tables each held a lamp with a diamond and leaf carved base, a gold, silver, and coppery metallic finish, and a stair-step footed platform base. Family pictures graced the end tables and walls.

Fred admired each photograph, one by one. When his eyes rested on the picture of his first grandchild, Kenji, sadness mixed with guilt overshadowed him. The photo of the one-year-old baby girl represented a missing link in the Smith family chain, and Fred knew he was the cause. Kenji was his son John's first daughter, born out of wedlock in Decatur, Georgia, with a girl, Shirley, he had met while in the Army. Liz and Shirley had become friends, writing letters to each other and exchanging pictures. At the time of baby Kenji's birth, Liz was twelve, and Shirley was seventeen.

"I would love for you to come down to Georgia this summer and spend time with me and the baby," Shirley had written.

"I would love to visit you in Georgia," Liz responded, "I just have to ask my parents."

When Liz approached her mother about the idea, Elsie's response had been, "No, you can't go to Georgia but tell her we'd be happy for her to come visit us."

When Fred heard the plan he objected. He had pulled Elsie aside to express his disapproval.

"I don't want that girl and her baby up here. She'd be a bad influence on my daughter," Fred had exclaimed.

"Oh, Fred, that's ridiculous. Becky is not going to come up pregnant just because John has a child," Elsie said, reviled by Fred's reasoning.

He continued to protest, and Elsie had eventually given up the fight but not because she had agreed with him. Elsie knew how nasty Fred could be. She would not subject Shirley and Kenji to Fred's ugly disposition nor would she allow him to embarrass her and Liz.

Fred's objections, whether he had realized it at the time, had been rooted in shame. Fred had grown up with the notion that a child born outside the sacred union of marriage was a shame on the family name. He would not have his family name marred by disgrace.

Fred focused on Kenji's picture and wondered for a brief moment how she was doing.

She'd be about seven or eight by now, he thought.

He finally looked away from the picture and returned to watching the television. The volume was turned down low.

"Someone must have turned it down while I was sleeping," Fred mumbled. "Yavonne," Fred called.

"Yes, Papa," Yavonne answered, leaping from her spot on the floor in front of Liz's bedroom door. She stood expectantly at the side of his chair waiting for Fred's request.

"Will you turn up the volume on the TV for Papa?"

"Okay."

After turning up the volume for Fred, Yavonne skipped back to her spot on the floor. Fred hoped the sound of the television would drown out the thoughts he was having about his first granddaughter. He didn't want to think about how her life was. Was she being properly cared for? Was she being abused? Was she getting enough to eat? He didn't want to think about his rejection of her and the reason for that rejection. He would never know what became of that little girl, his first granddaughter, Kenji. And he would never recognize the irony of his belief that her very existence would bring shame to his family name … just as his own grandfather had once believed about Fred.

Chapter 17

SOUTHPORT, NORTH CAROLINA

June 1920

Seven-year-old Fred Smith lagged behind the other children as the mass exodus of second graders exited Brunswick Elementary for the summer. He clutched his books and writing tablet tightly to his chest and looked toward the ground at his feet as he scuffed his shoes along the gravel road.

A cool breeze emanating from the Cape Fear River engulfed him, and he breathed in deeply, closing his eyes for a brief moment. As he exhaled, the tension in his body relaxed, and he released the firm grip he held on his books. A sensitive boy, Fred had been taken aback by his mother's sudden assertion that he could no longer sleep with her in her bed. He recalled the night before. He'd just finished with his bath when she had informed him of their new sleeping arrangements.

"From now on, Freddie, you sleep over there," his mother, Fannie, had said gently, pointing at a cot positioned on the opposite side of the bedroom.

Fred had looked over at the cot in the corner of the room and then back at Fannie's big, cozy bed with the soft, quilted bedspread embroidered with geometric patterns and the fluffy goose down pillows. He looked up at his mother with utter perplexity. She smiled at him, had given him a light kiss on the forehead, and aimed him toward his new bed.

What did I do to make her put me out of her bed? Fred now thought as he strolled down the road. His eyes were beginning to mist when Fred's books and tablet suddenly flew out of his arms and onto the ground. Someone had knocked them away. Fred looked up to see brothers and neighborhood tormenters, Pete and Joe Braxton, circling him. They laughed hysterically, pointing and jeering at Fred.

"Ah, ha, bastard boy," Joe yelled.

Fred hated these boys. Although they were a little older than Fred, they were not as tall. They frequently ridiculed him about one thing or another. They were darker in skin color. Fred was lighter, so they sometimes called him "yellow boy" or "orange boy." They had course, kinky hair. Fred had a milder grade of long hair and wore braids, so they called him "sissy boy" or "girly girl."

Now what are they calling me? What's bastard boy supposed to mean? Fred thought.

"Hey, boy. Who's your momma?" Pete asked, looking down at Fred who was picking up his books from the ground. As Fred stood and faced the boys, he narrowed his eyes.

"Yeah, what's your momma's name?" Joe now asked Fred in a taunting manner.

"Fannie Smith," Fred finally replied. He was confused by the question. He wondered why the boys were asking what they already knew.

Pete and Joe now roared with laughter at Fred's response. They doubled over, holding their stomachs, slapping their knees, shaking their heads, and pointing at Fred.

Fred felt a knot forming in the pit of his stomach. His face felt flushed, and the edge of his lips began to turn down.

"You know that woman is too old to be your momma," Pete said smiling, showing his yellow-stained teeth.

"She is my momma," Fred yelled.

The boys' laughter continued.

"He just don't know, do he Joe?" Pete asked his brother, extending the mocking.

"He don't even know his own momma," Joe responded, shaking his head as if to say Fred should be ashamed.

Fred's frustration increased. He couldn't understand why these boys mocked something he knew in his heart was true. Fannie Smith was his mother. His family included Dora Smith, his sister, whom he called Doe-Doe, and his other sister, Alethia Smith, whom he called Dee-Dee. They all called Fannie, Momma. Fred wondered what these two boys were really trying to insinuate about his family.

"Shut up, Pete," Fred spat out, walking away from the boys.

"Shut up, Pete," Pete mocked Fred. "What are you going to do now, cry?"

"No, he's going to run home and tell his mommy," Joe joked.

The two boys began to run in the opposite direction. Traces of their laughter lingered in the distance. The brothers seemed to be in on some big secret, which alluded Fred.

His body automatically turned in the direction of his home. After a while, Fred looked back. Pete and Joe were completely out of sight. Fred ran the rest of the way home.

"Momma, Momma," Fred shouted as he entered his home on Nash Street. Fannie raced from the kitchen to the living room, wiping her hands on her apron.

"What in tarnation is all the ruckus about?" she asked.

"They said you're not my momma." Fred gulped in hard breaths.

Fannie's heart skipped a beat, but she contained her apprehension.

"Who said that?" She asked in a calm and even tone.

"Those ole mean Braxton boys, Pete and Joe. They asked me,

'Who's your momma?' and I said, 'Fannie Smith,' and they said, 'Aw, you know that woman is too old to be your momma,' and I said—"

"Slow down, Freddie," Fannie interrupted. "You're getting yourself all in a tizzy. What do them fool boys know anyway? Them two don't know their rooter from their tooter. Now ain't that right?"

She scratched Fred's tummy, tickling him. He giggled. Fannie always knew how to make him feel better.

"But Momma, they called me 'bastard boy.' What does that mean?"

Fannie bristled at this. She then placed both hands on Fred's shoulders and looked him square in the eyes.

"Now let me tell you one thing," she said with a serious expression on her face. "Don't you worry your little head about nothing that nobody in this town says? Don't let nobody's ugly words and mean names hurt you. You just let it roll off you like water off a duck's back, you understand?"

"Yes, ma'am," Fred affirmed, although he didn't always understand Fannie's idioms.

"You just remember this," she continued. "You got three strong, black women at your back. So you hold your head up high and walk like you've got a purpose. In fact, you strut like you a proud peacock. You hear me?"

A broad smile came over Fred's face like the sunrise.

"Yes, ma'am."

"Good. Now you go wash up for supper. I made some Hoppin' John and cornbread for you."

"Oh boy, my favorite," Fred squealed.

* * *

Fred paced back and forth in front of the house anxiously waiting for Fannie and Dora to come out. The three of them were going to take the one-mile walk down to the train station to meet Alethia, who was coming home from college for the summer. Fannie and Dora were extremely proud of Alethia. The first in the family to attend college, twenty-year-old Alethia was a liberal arts major at Smith College in Northampton, Massachusetts.

Come on let's go, Fred screamed in his head.

He clenched his fist and stomped his foot in an expression of his growing impatience with Fannie and Dora's tardiness. A clattering sound across the street distracted him. Fred looked up to see a prisoner in chains being led by the sheriff. This image terrified Fred. His home was directly across the street from the jailhouse. The man in chains wore filthy overalls with no shirt. His black boots seemed to be too big for his feet by the clopping sound they made with each step. The man's bloodshot, red, steely eyes made contact with Fred's. Fred shuddered.

"You don't want to do nothing to get yourself locked up in that there jail," he recalled Fannie telling him on a number of occasions. "So you need to be a good boy."

Once she had even arranged for him to see the jail on the inside. The sheriff had showed Fred around.

"You see here boy," the sheriff said. "This here jail has two cells." Fred looked at the cells and had seen that each accommodated four bunks, a commode, and a washbasin. The cells had been constructed of flatiron bars riveted together, and there had been graffiti drawn on the walls by the prisoners. The smell of the commodes was repugnant, and Fred had to cover his mouth and nose to keep from gagging. The thought of being locked up in a cage like an animal had struck fear in young Fred's heart every time he recollected that visit.

"Okay, we're ready to go," Fannie announced as she and Dora exited the house with a basket of food.

"Finally," Fred mumbled under his breath.

"Did you say something, Freddie?" Fannie asked.

"Er, no ma'am. I'm ready to go," he said nervously.

Fred led the way to the train station. He knew the route well.

The previous year Alethia had shipped Fred a bicycle by train. She had sent it in sections. The first shipment had been the handlebars, the second had been the frame, and the last had been the wheels. Fred had pestered the train conductor every Saturday for weeks, inquiring about any packages for him. When all the parts had finally arrived, he remembered his neighbor Mr. Frink assembled the bicycle for him.

Mr. Frink and his wife lived on the street behind him—Rhett Street. This was his friend and next-door neighbor Caroline Frink's older brother, George. George used to spend time with Fred. But the birth of his own baby daughter had eased Fred out of the picture.

"Slow down, Freddie. We have plenty of time," he heard Fannie call out to him.

He couldn't help it if they had short legs and little feet and couldn't keep up with him. At only seven years old, Fred was almost as tall as both Fannie and Dora. But Alethia was taller. She towered over both Fannie and Dora by a good six inches. Fred knew that he too would grow up to be tall like Alethia.

"Okay," Fred yelled back in response to Fannie. He slowed is pace and took in the sights, sounds, and smells of his little town. Southport was just miles away from where the Cape Fear River joined with the Atlantic Ocean, making it a vital stop for fisherman, small shipping vessels, and maritime travelers along the bordering Intracoastal Waterway.

Fred liked to hang out at the pier on the Cape Fear River but stayed far from the banks of it. When he was younger, Fannie told Fred the story about how her son Wilber had drowned while swimming in the Cape Fear. The river's undercurrents had been strong that day and had pulled Wilber down. He had been powerless to escape the river's treacherous underbelly.

"He didn't have permission to go swimming alone," Fannie had told Fred. "He was disobedient. You got to mine your elders, Freddie, or bad things could happen to you."

Both Fannie and Dora often conveyed stories to Fred, which contained consequences as a way to keep him in line.

As they neared the train station, Fred heard the whistle blowing in the distance.

"It's coming, Momma. It's coming. The train is coming," Fred squealed, running toward the station.

"I hear it chil'. Calm yourself. It'll take a while before everyone is off the train," Fannie said.

"He sure is excited to see Lethia, ain't he, Momma," Dora said.

"Yeah, chil', he sure is. So am I."

When Alethia exited the train, Fred was the first to greet her. To Fred, she looked regal, like a Nubian queen. She stood five foot, seven inches tall. She was slim and wore her long, thick hair in a bun positioned at the nape of her long neck. She wore a plain blue ankle-length dress, black ankle-strapped, button shoes, and a straw hat.

"Dee-Dee," Fred screamed running toward her.

"Aw Freddie," Alethia said with outstretched arms to receive the little boy.

Fred folded into Alethia's arms. She lifted his long thin body off the ground, and he wrapped his legs around her waist.

"I missed you so much," she whispered while kissing him on the ear.

She twisted her body from side to side swinging Fred with her. Fred squeezed tighter and nestled his face deeper into his sister's neck.

"I missed you too," he whispered.

"Okay, quit hogging her all to yourself," Fannie said, breaking the spell between the two. "Other people want a hug too."

Fred and Alethia released their embrace, and she dropped the boy to his feet.

"You're getting so tall," Alethia said to Fred, rubbing the top of his head. She then turned her attention to Fannie.

"Hello Momma. You look well. I'm so happy to see you." Alethia bent down to kiss her mother and then gave her a tender hug.

She then turned to her older sister, Dora. They embraced. "Hello, sister," Alethia said.

"Hi, Lethia. You're looking well.

"Thank you."

"Momma brought some food. You hungry?"

Alethia looked over at her mother. "Oh, Momma, thank you," she exclaimed. "Yes, Dora, I'm famished."

"Let's go outside to the back of the train station to eat," Dora suggested.

"Okay, and you all can catch me up on what's been going on around this sleepy town since my last visit," Alethia said.

"Well, that won't take long," Dora joked.

The three women erupted into laughter and exited the building with Fred following close behind.

Chapter 18

JUNE 1925

Twelve-year-old Fred sat on his back porch, one warm Thursday evening when he heard the sound of a baby crying. His back porch was cater-cornered from the back porch of his neighbor's, George Frink. Fred leaped to his feet when he saw Mr. Frink's sister Jessie step out onto the back porch to empty a pan of water.

"Evening, Miss Jessie," Fred yelled, waving in the woman's direction. "I heard a baby crying. Is it a girl or a boy?"

"It's a girl," the woman responded politely and returned inside.

A lot had changed in Fred's family dynamic during the last five years, and he was not at all comfortable with it. In 1922, Alethia had earned her liberal arts degree and was teaching in upstate New York. She hadn't been back home to visit since that summer in 1920. She couldn't be bound to the confines of a small sea town like Southport. She loved being up north, with all its boundless possibilities.

Dora, too had become restless. All her life she had been the good and dutiful daughter, sticking by Momma's side all those years after her father and brother had died unexpectedly just months apart. At thirty-four years old, Dora had decided that she too wanted to branch out on her own a bit. So she had taken a domestic job in nearby Wilmington, North Carolina, as a live-in cook and housekeeper, the year before. Fred had been heartbroken by her decision to leave home. He had felt abandoned and had worried about how he and Fannie would survive without her.

Fannie worked long hours as a clothes presser at a laundry business. At the age of fifty-four, she held her own against others who were much younger. Many nights after returning home from a long, hard day at work, she had simply been too tired to cook dinner for herself and Fred.

On these occasions, she'd send Fred to the store for a block of cheese and Johnny Cakes—sometimes called stage planks—which were old-fashioned gingerbread cookies with a layer of flavored icing on top. Fred had enjoyed these treats. However, Fannie knew that long hours left alone after school and sugary treats for dinner were not healthy for a growing impressionable boy. It was during this time that George Frink and his wife stepped in to help.

* * *

Fred finished his evening meal at the Frink's home and began washing and rinsing the dishes while their daughter, Georgia, whom everyone called Inez, dried the dishes and put them away. Mr. Frink had adjourned to the parlor to read the evening newspaper while his wife tended to their baby, Louise. When the grandfather clock struck seven, Fred knew that Fannie would be home, and it was time for him to leave.

"Thank you, Mrs. Frink, for the delicious meal," Fred said entering the parlor.

"You're quite welcome, Fred," she responded, holding the wiggling baby in her arms.

The child always seemed to light up when she saw Fred. He smiled at the baby and gently pinched her chubby cheeks. He then turned his attention to Mr. Frink, whose newspaper nearly covered his entire face.

"Thank you for dinner, sir," Fred said, standing in front of him as straight as an arrow. Mr. Frink lowered the paper but never diverted his eyes from its contents.

"Did you get enough to eat?" He said in a baritone voice.

"Yes, sir."

"Okay then, we'll see you tomorrow.

"Good night, sir."

Fred exited the house through the back door and hopped the fence. When he entered his house, he saw that Fannie was fast asleep on the sofa.

She works so hard, he thought.

He went into the bedroom, which was now vacated by Dora, and sprawled himself across the bed facedown. His stomach was full from the wonderful meal Mrs. Frink had prepared, and he was satisfied, but only in the physical sense.

He yearned to be a part of a family unit like the Frink family, with a father figure at the helm, a mother, who was a homemaker, and siblings. Up to this point, Fred had led a somewhat sheltered and isolated life. He had few friends and had spent the majority of his time in the company of adults. He was well mannered. People liked him, but his social skills were lacking. His deficiency in self-esteem and self-confidence stemmed from the absence of a steady male father figure in his life. This deficiency would soon be filled by a less than qualified character named Hun Taylor.

Chapter 19

SOUTHPORT, NORTH CAROLINA

July 1929

Fred ran toward the back fence and then hoisted his body up. His long legs glided over the fence gracefully and carried him into the Frink's backyard. His feet made a thudding sound upon landing. He climbed the four steps of the Frink's back porch, two at a time. He tapped on the windowpane of the back door. Inez opened the door to greet him.

"Hi, Freddie."

"Hey, Nez," Fred said, stepping over the threshold. He walked through the dining room into the living room where four-year-old Louise sat on the shiny hardwood floor playing with a rag doll.

"Hi, Weezie," Fred called out to the little girl.

When she saw Fred, Louise sprang to her feet and took off running toward him still clutching the doll. "Freddie," she squealed.

Just before she reached Fred, Louise leaped from the floor into his arms. Fred caught her. The force knocked the wind from his chest and sent him into a tailspin. They both spun around. Louise laughed. This had become a ritual between the two each time he came to the house. Fred's appearance seemed to bring the child joy, and her response made him feel blissful inside. He gave her a gentle squeeze and a soft peck on her chubby cheeks before lowering her back to the floor.

"What you got there?" Fred asked the child.

She held up her doll to show Fred. "Dolly," she responded.

"Aw, she's pretty, but not as pretty as you," Fred said looking down at the child with adoring eyes.

Louise smiled and skipped back to her spot across the room. Fred took a seat on the sofa and waited for the rest of the family.

It was first Sunday. He was going to attend services at Saint James Methodist Church, where Reverend Samuel Frink, George Frink's father, was pastor. Fred attended Reverend Frink's church once a month and every Easter and Christmas.

He especially looked forward to having Sunday dinner after church with George Frink's family. While he waited, Fred's mind began to think on how much things had changed in his own family dynamic. They were changes that made him feel uncomfortable and powerless.

Earlier that year, while still in Wilmington, North Carolina, Dora had sent a cablegram to Fannie saying that she had met a man named Wiley Taylor, whom she called Hun, which was short for Honey. Three months later, Dora and Hun had been married in a civil ceremony and had relocated to Norfolk, Virginia. They had planned to come to Southport for a visit at the end of July.

Two years prior, while in college, Alethia had married a man she'd met in Nantucket, Massachusetts, named Francis Pasterisk, whom she called Boy. In a letter, she had told Fred that she called him Boy because Francis sounded like a girl's name to her. The two had lived in New York for years now. Although Alethia had written to Fred and had sent him gifts over the many years that she'd been gone, Fred missed her physical presence terribly. His mother, Fannie, while physically present became more emotionally distant to him.

Fred noticed the change in Fannie after she'd had a dispute with Miss Sarah the previous summer. Not one to place her trust in banks, Fannie had asked the white woman to hold onto her savings for her. Every week for nearly a year, Fannie had given Miss Sarah a nickel, a dime, or a quarter to hold for her.

Fannie Berry had known Miss Sarah Jenkins for many years. When Fannie was fifteen, and Sarah was ten, Fannie had lived with the Jenkins' family. She had been charged with taking care of Sarah's elderly grandmother, Sadie, who had shown signs of dementia. Fannie's job had been to bath Sadie, feed her, and keep an eye on her, as Sadie had a habit of wandering away from home and getting lost.

Fannie was eighteen when Sadie died. One part of Fannie's life had ended with Sadie's death, but another chapter had begun when Fannie married her beau, Romeo Smith, a local boy, who had worked on his father's farm.

After all those years of knowing Sarah, Fannie had felt that she could trust her. Fred had been with Fannie the day she had asked Sarah for her money.

"Morning, Miss Sarah," Fannie called from the bottom of the steps. Sarah sat in a white wicker rocking chair on her wraparound porch wearing a wide-brimmed, peach-colored hat and sipping ice tea.

"Morning, Fannie," Sarah replied. "What brings you around here?"

"I come for my money," Fannie replied proudly, thinking that she should have quite a nest egg by now.

"What money?" Sarah replied in a nonchalant manner.

"The money I been giving to you to hold for me all these months. What you mean 'What money?'" Fannie had felt heat creep up her spine.

"Don't you take that tone with me, gal. Who do you think

you are talking to?" Sarah spat out as if she had been the wronged person.

Fannie cast her eyes to the ground as she had remembered her Negro skin and therefore, her station in life. Regardless that she had been five years older than this white woman, Fannie had to cower to this apparent thief.

Fannie had quickly softened her facial expression. When she looked back up, she tilted her head to the left, exposing her jugular as a nonverbal sign of submission. She twisted a powder-blue handkerchief that had once belonged to her late husband, Romeo, around her fingers and invoked a childlike voice.

"Er, sorry ma'am. I don't mean you no disrespect. But don't you remember me asking you to hold my money for me on account of I don't trust the bank to hold it for me? You said you'd be glad to help me out. I'm in powerful need of that money now Miss."

Sarah looked toward the floor of the porch. Her facial expression had been stoic. Several seconds had gone by before a word had passed between the two women. Sarah inhaled deeply and then released the air with great exasperation.

"I don't remember no sucha thing," Sarah finally said.

Fannie's face felt flushed. The pit of her stomach felt like a fiery cauldron had just bubbled over. She had thought she felt the steam ascend up her body and burst out of every orifice in her head. Fannie had closed her eyes, momentarily, trying desperately to maintain her composure. She exhaled, blowing the air through the small hole she had formed with her lips.

"Miss Sarah," Fannie finally said, "I been bringing you my hard earned nickels, dimes, and quarters for months now, saving for a raining day. I needs my money now, Miss."

Sarah had risen from her rocking chair. She held onto a porch beam to steady herself.

"I don't know what you're talking about, gal. Now go on home and leave me alone."

Sarah had gone inside her house and closed the door behind her, leaving a bewildered Fannie standing on the sidewalk empty-handed.

She ain't never been right after that, Fred thought. He was jolted from his memories when he heard George Frink's voice.

"Okay, are we all ready to leave?"

"Yes, Poppa," Inez said, responding for everyone.

"Fine. Well let's go then. We don't want to be late," George said, exiting the house with the others following in lockstep.

Fred liked attending church, but he was glad that he didn't have to attend on a regular basis. Because she worked most Sunday's, Fannie didn't attend church herself but wanted to make sure Fred did. So she asked the Frinks if Fred could go with them from time to time.

Fred subscribed to the general Christian philosophy of love thy neighbor and the belief that all good people went to heaven, but services at Saint James were long, and Reverend Frink tended to deliver long-winded sermons. Fred had a short attention span and struggled to stay awake during the delivery of the message. He sat as straight as he could on the highly-polished, slippery, mahogany, wooden pew.

Although his eyes were open, a thin gray veil seemingly came out of nowhere. It blurred his vision and seemed to shut down his brain activity. His hearing began to fade like the volume of a radio being lowered. Reverend Frink's voice sounded just above a whisper. But an old familiar word shook Fred out of his semi-sleep state.

"A bastard shall not enter into the congregation of the Lord, even to his tenth generation shall he not enter into the congregation of the Lord." Reverend Frink read from the twenty-third chapter of the book of Deuteronomy.

Fred recalled the Braxton brothers calling him "bastard boy."

His mother told him that they didn't know what they were talking about and not to pay them any attention.

It sounded like a bad thing when the Braxton brothers said it, Fred thought. *Now here Reverend Frink is reading out of the Bible, and it still sounds like a bad thing.*

Chapter 20

Fred met Dora and Hun at the train station. At first glance, Fred immediately thought Dora and her new husband looked like an odd pairing. He compared them to the comic strip *Mutt and Jeff.*

Dora had changed in the four years since Fred had last seen her. Gone was the thin, petite, wide-eyed woman that he remembered. She had added quite a bit of weight to her five-foot, one-inch frame. She appeared to be as wide as she was tall. The darkened saddle bags under her eyes from apparent lack of sleep made her look older than the additional four years she'd aged.

Hun Taylor was nearly a foot taller than Dora and had a big rounded belly that shook each time he laughed, which was often. Fred was immediately turned off by his appearance. He wore blue overalls that were covered with paint splatters and a little white cap, which sat on the back of his head with its brim pointed directly toward the sky.

After a week, Fred was eager for Dora and her new husband's visit to be over. He loved Dora, but this guy was too rude and crude for Fred's liking.

"He will just walk across the room and pass gas in front of Momma and Dora and won't even say excuse me," Fred complained to his next-door neighbor and classmate, Caroline Frink, while walking together from the store and drinking Orange Crush sodas.

"So how long are they here for?" Caroline asked.

"I don't know," Fred replied, crinkling his nose and rolling his eyes. "Doe said she has something to tell me when I get back. I hope it's that they are leaving."

"Aw, why would you say that? I thought you would be happy to have Dora home."

"I am. I just don't care for her husband."

"Why, what's wrong with him?"

"Well, for one thing, he's uneducated."

"Oh, can't he read?"

"Yeah, but just barely."

"So, how does he make a living? Does he at least have a trade?"

"He's a painter, if you can call that a trade. The work seems to be scarce, because he's been unemployed longer than employed. Doe looks so run-down and tired. I think she's carrying more of the load than him," Fred said disgusted. He took another swig of his soda.

As the two friends approached Fred's house, Fred saw Hun in the window.

"They must be waiting for me."

"Okay, well, I'll see you around," Caroline said waving.

"See you later," Fred said.

When Fred entered the house, Fannie and Dora were seated on the sofa.

"Have a seat, Fred," Dora said pointing to the chair that was positioned across from the sofa. "There's something I need to tell you."

The look on Dora's face worried Fred. He sat down in the chair.

"Where's Hun?" Fred asked.

"He's in the kitchen," Dora said.

Fred looked at Fannie, who was not making eye contact with him. Her hands were folded in her lap, and her eyes remained down. As Dora began to speak, her voice quivered.

"Fred, there is so much that you need to know about our family. I just don't know where to begin. We should have told you years ago," Dora said looking at her mother.

Fred's eyes darted back and forth, first to Dora and then to Fannie. He tried to gage the expression on their faces in a futile attempt to guess the big revelation.

"Er, son, when I was younger I made a mistake," Dora began.

Why did she call me son? She never called me that before. Fred leaned forward in the chair and listened intently.

"You see," she continued, "I had a child out of wedlock." She paused to assess Fred's reaction to this. His face remained stoic as he rested his cheek in his hand. "I had a baby boy, Fred. You are my son."

Fred's eyes narrowed. He had a million questions racing through his head. He had a burning sensation in his chest that felt as if it had traveled to his throat and had stuck there. He opened his mouth, but no words came out. He coughed and cleared his throat.

"So if you're my mother," Fred said pointing to Dora and trying not to strangle on his own saliva, "then you're my—" Fred turned to look at Fannie who interrupted his statement.

"Grandmother," she said, looking up and locking eyes with the confused teenager.

"Yes, and Alethia's your aunt," Dora interjected.

The pages of the book of Fred's short life flipped fast in his mind. He remembered the Braxton boys taunting him about who his mother was. Their words, "He just don't know, do he?" came to mind and, "That woman is too old to be your momma." Fred felt flushed. He tugged at his collar and then leaned back in the chair. It was all too much for him to take in, but he had to hear it all.

"So, who is my father?" Fred asked somewhat reluctantly. There was silence in the room. Fred watched as Dora and Fannie looked at each other for several seconds. Dora finally turned her attention back to Fred.

"George Frink," she finally said.

Fred gasped and covered his mouth with his hand for a moment. Then he clenched his jaws. Ambivalence settled in his spirit. On one hand, it was his greatest wish come true—to be a member of what he believed was the ideal family. Soon though, his brief moment of glee faded when he felt compelled to ask her the obvious question.

"Does he know I'm his son?" Fred wasn't sure if he wanted to know the answer.

"Yes, he knows," Fannie interjected. Dora and Fannie held hands and looked at each other for a moment.

Fannie began to speak. "Well, chil', it's like this. George wanted to do the right thing and marry Dora when he found out you was on the way. But he was already betrothed to the woman he's married to now—Veitha."

"What's betrothed?" Fred asked.

"It means they were promised to each other," Fannie said. Suddenly, Fred came to a realization that struck his body like a bolt of lightning. He raised his hands revealing his palms.

"Wait a minute," he exclaimed. Fred craned his neck forward as his moist eyes darted back and forth between the two women. "Are y'all telling me that not only is George Frink my father, but Inez and Louise are my sisters?"

Before anyone could respond, Fred leapt to his feet. He'd just made the connection with the word bastard as the Braxton boys used it and what he heard in church on first Sunday.

"And Reverend Frink," Fred yelled while pointing in the direction of the man's house next door, "who preaches about bastards not entering the congregation with the Lord, what did he have to say about all this?" Fred demanded looking down on the two petite women sitting on the sofa.

"He told George to marry Veitha," Dora said looking down at the floor.

Fred paced back and forth in front of the sofa. His head was spinning. He massaged his temples, trying to process the flood of new information about his paternity.

"So all Reverend Frinks' children—Annie, Evelyn, Grace, Emmitt, John, Jessie, Cora, and even Caroline—are my aunts and uncles. Do they know? Does Caroline know?"

"All of them know except Caroline," Dora said looking up at Fred teary-eyed. "Me and George's momma, Louisa, was pregnant at the same time."

Fred felt as though the walls had begun to close around him. It was as if all the air in the room had been sucked out. He couldn't breathe.

"I gotta get out of here," Fred said.

He ran out the front door and kept running until he reached the pier. He sat on the pier crying until dusk and then returned home just before sunset. When he entered the house, he was greeted by Fannie.

"You want something to eat chil'?" she asked.

Fred was sick to his stomach. Food was the last thing on his mind.

"No, I just want to go to bed," Fred whispered.

He entered his room and lay on the bed. He was exhausted, and sleep came within minutes. He needed his rest. Fred didn't know it in that moment, but more life-changing news would come in the morning.

Chapter 21

NORFOLK, VIRGINIA

October 1930

After waiting almost twenty minutes for old man Kruger to finish serving all the white customers, Fred finally purchased the pound of lard Dora had asked him to pick up from the market after school.

When he was ready to exit the store, he proceeded with caution. He stepped outside and peered down the street in both directions. When the coast seemed clear, he began to walk briskly down the street. He nervously looked over his shoulder and took longer and faster strides. Fred tucked the bag containing the lard under his arm and began to think about how much he hated living in Norfolk—not so much the city itself but his living situation.

Dora was married to shiftless Hun Taylor. She had brought Fred and Fannie to Virginia to live with them on O'Keefe Street. On the one hand, Fred was relieved to have left Southport in the midst of learning about his father. He was outraged that he had not been openly acknowledged as a Frink and not even considered good enough to carry the Frink surname. But despite his anger, he didn't have the courage to face any of them again after learning the truth—not Inez, not Caroline, and especially not George Frink.

Fred was enrolled in Booker T. Washington High School. He found the school to be rowdy with kids running through the halls, yelling and cursing. Most of the boys did not like the tall, slim, good-looking newcomer. However, most of the girls found Fred attractive, with his fine, textured hair, light-brown skin tone, and dreamy eyes crowned with long eyelashes.

One boy that took an immediate dislike to Fred was a school bully, whom everyone called Black Ricky. Ricky was a husky boy about six inches shorter than Fred was. Ricky wanted to fight Fred and chased him just about every day after school. However, Ricky's short stocky build was no match for catching the slim, swift Fred, who could run as fast as a gazelle.

Fred stopped at the intersection of a busy street waiting for the traffic to clear before crossing. When he heard a familiar voice behind him, he cringed.

"Is that pretty boy Smith I see?"

Black Ricky approached Fred from behind. Fred looked around to see Ricky sneering at him.

Shit, Fred thought as he began running down the street.

Ricky took off in close pursuit. Ricky reached out to grab Fred's shirttail but missed. Fred propelled his chest forward, pumping his arms while still maintaining his hold on the bag of lard now in his right hand. He made a quick left on a street that he was familiar with. It was in a white neighborhood, and he was sure Ricky would stop his pursuit of him and not enter the area. But he was wrong.

Ricky was undaunted and continued the chase even though Fred had widened his lead considerably. Fred approached the home of Mark Weisberg, an attorney for whom Dora housecleaned three days a week. Fred often met Dora at the back door of Mr. Weisberg's house after work to walk her home.

When he reached the house, he placed his left hand on the fence and hoisted his body over with ease. It took him one leap over the three short steps to reach the front porch. While standing at the screen door, Fred noticed the front door of the house was slightly open. Before he could knock on the screen door, he heard Ricky's voice call out to him from a distance.

"Where you think you're going, you son of a bitch," Ricky said approaching the house.

Fred looked back at Ricky who was charging toward the house like a bull. Without thinking, Fred snatched opened Mr. Weisberg's screen door and entered the house closing the front door behind him.

"What in the hell?" Fred heard Mr. Weisberg say as he jumped from his dinner table. He rushed into the living room to see Fred standing at the front door clutching the bag of lard at his chest while trying to catch his breath. He was sweating profusely.

"Fred Smith, what do you think you're doing running into my house like this?"

"Sorry, sir," Fred replied breathless. "That boy outside has been chasing me. He's trying to beat me up." Fred wiped the sweat dripping down his face with his hand.

"What boy?" Mr. Weisberg asked.

"He's right outside your house sir. His name is Ricky. I know him from school. He's always trying to fight me." Mr. Weisberg pulled back the door curtain to see a boy much shorter than Fred pacing back and forth in front of his house.

"Do you mean to tell me you've been running from that little boy?" Mr. Weisberg exclaimed.

Fred was speechless. He had no justifiable response to Mr. Weisberg's question that would have been acceptable. The truth was that Fred was not a confrontational person. He avoided conflict at all costs, and he didn't know how to stand up for himself. If he had the ability to stand up to people he detested like Hun Taylor, he wouldn't have run so much.

"Yes, sir," Fred finally said. Mr. Weisberg opened the door and stepped out on the porch. Fred stayed inside. Suddenly, he felt a presence still in the room. He looked over toward the dining room to see Mr. Weisberg's wife and two young daughters standing in the doorway.

"Oh, afternoon, ma'am," Fred said to the woman while nodding his head. She crinkled her nose and placed her hands on each of her daughters' shoulders leading them back into the dining room.

"Now you get on out of this neighborhood before I call the police and have you hauled away for trespassing," Fred heard Mr. Weisberg tell Black Ricky. Fred peeked out the doorway to see Ricky leaving and Mr. Weisberg returning inside.

"All right, Fred, that little hoodlum is gone. Now you get on home and make that the last time you ever run into my house like that again."

"Yes, sir," Fred said exiting the man's home. Once outside, he looked around for signs of Ricky.

Ricky must have taken Mr. Weisberg's threat about calling the police seriously, Fred thought.

When Fred got home and entered the house, he saw Hun in the living room. He was napping in his brown overstuffed chair. Fred quietly closed the front door and attempted to tiptoe by without waking Hun.

"Boy, what the hell took you so long?" Hun said, startling Fred.

"Er, I had to wait a really long time until Mr. Kruger finished waiting on all the white folks," Fred embellished.

"Well your momma is waiting on that there lard to fry me some chicken."

Fred bristled at this. *Who in the hell does this shiftless bastard think he is? She's frying chicken for all of us, you lazy son of a bitch,* Fred shouted within himself.

Hun resented Fred, and he resented Fred's appetite. If Fred ate more than one piece of chicken, which he often did, Hun would scowl at him, contorting his lips.

"Damn boy, I'd rather clothe you than feed you," Hun often said to Fred at the dinner table.

You don't clothe me or feed me, so I don't know what the hell you're even talking about, Fred screamed in his head, looking across the table at Hun with piercing eyes.

"You got to get yourself a job, boy. You old enough to start helping bring some money in this house."

Fred resented Hun's assertions and felt hurt that Dora didn't stand up for him. He also hated how Hun took Dora for granted.

I know she could have done better than this man. What in the world does she see in him? Fred asked himself.

*   *   *

In March 1931, Fred obtained a part-time job after school as a porter at Masters Pharmacy on the corner of Colley and Princess Anne Road. He had been there to pick up medicine for Fannie, who had been ailing.

"I'm sorry Dr. Masters, suh," Fred overheard a young man saying to the store owner. "I got me a porter job over at Central Pharmacy pays more than I'm making here. I got me a wife to support now."

"You're leaving me in the lurch, Noah," Dr. Masters said.

"I know, and I'm sorry 'bout that, suh," the young man replied leaving the store.

"Shit," Dr. Master said under his breath.

Fred thought that the sudden job opening was an opportunity that he could not pass up. Nervous, Fred approach the store owner.

"Excuse me, sir. I couldn't help but overhear that gentleman is quitting his job here."

"Yes, and damn thoughtless of him not even giving me sufficient notice," Dr. Masters said in a huff.

"Well, sir, I'm a sophomore at Booker T. High. I'd be willing to work for you after school and during the summer."

A relieved look came over Dr. Masters' face.

"That sounds like a fine proposal. What's your name, boy?"

"John Frederick Smith, sir, but everybody calls me Fred."

"Well, Fred, you seem like a good kid. I'm going to give you a trial period. You work for me for free for a week. If I like what I see, you're hired. How's that sound?"

"That sounds fine, sir."

"Okay, so when can you start?"

"I can start today, sir, soon as I run this medicine home to my grandmother."

Fred worked at Masters Pharmacy through the end of August that year. But when Fred returned to school in September, Dr. Masters had hired someone else to work full time.

The little bit of money he had contributed had helped with the groceries, which had been one of Hun's main complaints. But ironically, later that month, Hun would add another mouth to feed to their multigenerational family unit.

One Sunday after church, Dora, Fred, and Fannie returned home to find a six-year-old boy on Hun's lap in the living room. They were listening to the radio.

"Whose child is that?" Dora asked, looking bewildered.

"This here is little Jimmy," Hun said in a nonchalant manner. "His momma gave him to us. Said she had too many kids and can't afford to feed them all."

Fred stood behind Dora clenching his teeth. He couldn't believe what he was seeing and hearing.

Just when I thought this man couldn't be any more selfish or inconsiderate, he brings another mouth home to feed, Fred thought. He was seething. *Of all the things that Dora has put up with, this takes the cake.*

Fred recalled the time when Hun and Dora had been saving money by throwing all their spare change on top of the wardrobe in their bedroom. After several months, Dora had figured that there should have been quite a bit of money up there. After all, she had been faithfully tossing coins up every other week.

One particularly hot summer day, she had wanted to treat Fred and herself to ice cream cones. So she had asked Fred to get twenty-five cents down for them. But when Fred had climbed onto a chair to see on top of the six-foot-high wardrobe, there hadn't been a single coin up there. Hun had been taking the money for himself. The look on Dora's face crushed Fred to his core. It had reminded him of the time Miss Sarah had taken Fannie's money back in Southport. Once again, he had felt powerless to do anything about the situation.

He also remembered a day he had been helping Dora clean the living room. He had stumbled upon a gold-colored lingerie box under the sofa, where he'd been sweeping. When he showed it to Dora, she'd assumed it was a present for her since she had a birthday coming up. She hadn't been able to resist taking a peek inside the box. But joyous anticipation had soon turned to disappointment when she found a pair of white, laced underpants three sizes too big for Dora to fit in.

Fred had quickly surmised that Hun had bought the lingerie for another woman. Fred fumed at the blatant disrespect Hun had shown his mother. But at the same time, he had also been disappointed that Dora chose to put the box back in its hiding place and not confront Hun about it.

Surely this would be just cause for her to throw the no-good bastard out of the house, Fred thought, but she did nothing. Now he had brought some stray child home without consulting anyone about it first.

"Are you kidding me?" Fred blurted out, not realizing for a second that he'd actually asked the question out loud.

Hun shot Fred a disparaging look. "What did you say?" Hun asked getting up from his seat.

Dora interrupted. "Hun, I don't understand. What do you

mean she gave him to you?" Dora asked, diverting his attention away from Fred.

"I told you, she has too many children that she can't afford to take care of, so she gave him to us. What don't you understand, woman?"

"Come into the bedroom with me, Hun. We need to talk about this in private."

Hun plopped little Jimmy on the chair and followed Dora into their bedroom. After they were gone, Fannie went over to the little boy. She rubbed his head as Jimmy looked up at the old woman with his sad little eyes.

"You hungry, sugah?"

The little boy nodded.

"Well, Grand Momma Fannie's gonna fix us all something to eat."

Fannie exited the room and entered the kitchen, leaving Fred alone with Jimmy. Fred sat down on the sofa across from the child. He noticed that the boy's shoelaces were untied. He placed Jimmy's little feet on his lap and tied the child's white high-top, walking shoes for him. Little Jimmy's sad eyes turned bright, and he smiled at Fred. Fred smiled back. A warm feeling engulfed him—a feeling that he hadn't felt in years.

"So how old are you," Fred asked the tike.

"Six," Jimmy replied, eager to please.

Fred thought of Louise who would also be six by now. He realized that he missed Inez and Louise, his half-sisters. He regretted that he hadn't said good-bye. He wished he'd taken the opportunity to tell them that they were family and that he loved them. He missed how Louise lit up when he entered the Frink home and how she leapt into his arms each time she saw him. Perhaps little Jimmy's arrival was a blessing in disguise after all. Maybe through this child, Fred could recapture that blissful feeling he had gotten when he was around his little sisters back in Southport.

* * *

By 1937, Fred had been working as a porter at Central Pharmacy on Colonial Avenue. He'd dropped out of high school after completing the eleventh grade. Although working full time and bringing in money for the family, the tension between Fred and Hun grew with each passing year.

At the age of twenty-four, Fred knew the time had long passed for him to move out. However, the money he earned at Central Pharmacy did not pay well enough for Fred to afford his own place. But as fate would have it, a rare opportunity for Fred was on the horizon.

"Fred, can you come out here?" his boss, Mr. Berman, called out to Fred, who was working in the storage room.

"Yes, sir, what do you need?" Fred replied emerging from the back of the store.

"I just got off the telephone with my Richmond branch manager. I own a Standard Drug there. Anyway, they need a porter to work the first shift, and I think you'd be perfect for the job."

"First shift, sir?" Fred asked perplexed.

"Yes, you'd work from four in the morning to twelve noon, and get this, the job comes with a private room over the store, rent free."

Fred thought he felt his eyes just protrude out of his head. Did he hear Mr. Berman correctly? A new job in another city an hour away with free room and board?

"If you're interested, the job is yours," Mr. Berman said. "All you have to do is purchase your own bus ticket to Richmond. Mr. Lott will pick you up from the Greyhound terminal."

Fred's heart was beating a mile a minute. He was so excited and could hardly wait to get home to tell his family the good news.

Fred began work at the Standard Drug Company in Richmond,

The World outside Our Door 153

Virginia, in December of 1937. The store was huge. It even had a lunch counter. It was on the colored side of that lunch counter where Fred first saw his future wife, a beautiful young woman named Lillian Corbin.

Chapter 22

RICHMOND, VIRGINIA

March 1938

As soon as the red second hand on the clock swept the number twelve, Fred's shift ended for the day. It was noon, and he dropped his push broom and hurried up the stairs at the back of the store, which led to his dwelling on the second floor.

The small room, with its pale blue-gray painted walls was modestly furnished. On one side of the room, there was a lumpy twin-sized mattress on a wooden-slatted bed frame and a pinewood, bedside nightstand. The matching four-drawer-high chest was donned with a radio on top. On the other side of the room, a card table and folding chair served as his dining area. The bathroom was equipped with a sink and a toilet but no bathtub.

Fred entered the room and immediately began to disrobe. He went into the bathroom and began to wash up. His heartbeat increased as his excitement grew in anticipation of seeing the lovely, young woman, who came into the store for lunch every day. Fred had been smitten with her at first sight.

She was a petite little thing about five-foot-two, with long, black hair, skin the color of peanut butter, and brownish-green eyes that, to Fred, looked like two hazel nuts staring back at him. She worked as a part-time clerk at the local department store handing out perfume samples to customers. For the last month and a half, the only time Fred was able to spend time with her was during her lunch hour.

As he finished shaving, Fred gazed at himself in the mirror. *I sure would like to spend some time with her away from the store,* he thought.

She was mysterious to him, never giving away too much about herself and never accepting his requests to take her out on a date.

Fred grabbed the towel from the rack and wiped the residual shaving cream off his face. He then slapped on some aftershave cologne.

I can't believe they just throw this stuff away, Fred thought, recalling the first time his boss had told him to destroy a box of sample products. That box had contained all colors of lipstick. His boss had told Fred to pour paint all over them to make sure no one could use them. *Damn wasteful,* he thought.

The next time his boss told Fred to destroy sample products, it had been several bottles of perfume and cologne. Before doing so, Fred pocketed a few for himself. The first time he had snaffled some products, he had felt guilty.

Don't ever do nothing that might land you in that there jail, he had remembered his grandmother Fannie telling him when he was a little boy. He had shrugged his shoulders and sucked in his breath. *Shit, this store would rather throw this stuff away than let somebody have it, so it can't be stealing,* he had justified.

Fred put on a fresh shirt and gave himself one more look in the mirror before heading out the door and descending back down to the store. He entered the store from the rear and walked toward the lunch counter. Lillian always arrived by 12:15 pm and sat in that same seat at the counter. But today, she wasn't there. His heart sank. He peered around the huge store in hopes of catching a glimpse of her in the vicinity. He began to walk around. He looked down each aisle. His disappointment started to settle down in the pit of his stomach. He was hungry but couldn't eat. He knew the nervous quiver in his gut wouldn't allow any food to come down and settle in.

I could go for a taste, Fred thought.

It had become a habit of his since coming to Richmond. At first he had only drunk a glass of wine to help him fall asleep. Then he had begun drinking sherry when he had felt anxious or unsure of himself. Drinking calmed his angst.

"Looking for someone," a voice said behind him.

Fred immediately recognized the melodic voice. He turned and saw her. It was Lillian. He was so excited that a lump formed in his throat.

"Hey, I thought you weren't coming today," Fred managed to utter.

"I didn't make it to work today," Lillian said avoiding Fred's eyes.

"Oh, why not?"

"Er, I just had something to take care of," she said.

Fred sensed that whatever it was, Lillian didn't want to talk about it so he decided not to pursue it any further.

"So, if you're not going to work today, do you want to get some sandwiches and sodas and walk over to the park and eat lunch?" Fred asked expectedly.

Lillian looked up at Fred and smiled. She was silent for several seconds before she answered. "Yes, I'd love to."

Fred exhaled and felt a sense of relief in his entire body.

Yes, she finally agreed to spend time with me outside of this store, he thought.

Fred took Lillian by the hand and led her over to the lunch counter. His touch startled her, but she relaxed and allowed him to escort her.

"What y'all having?" the cook asked Fred.

Fred turned and looked at Lillian. "What would you like?" he asked.

Lillian smiled sheepishly. "I'd like a tuna sandwich and orange soda," she answered.

"That sounds great. We'll have two tuna sandwiches and two orange sodas," Fred said to the cook. "And can you wrap them up? We're eating at the park."

The cook gave Fred a knowing wink. "You got it," he said.

At the park, Fred smiled as he watched Lillian peel off the crust of her sandwich and toss it to the pigeons and other birds. A squirrel approached them and gave an inquisitive look. It twitched its nose and stood on its hind limbs. Lillian broke off a piece of her sandwich and tossed it to the bushy-tailed rodent.

She leaned back where Fred's right arm was stretched out on the back of the bench. When her body touched his arm, Fred gently caressed her shoulder. Lillian gazed straight ahead, and Fred watched her mood change from a look of serenity, to being in a daze, to a look of sadness, which shadowed her face.

"What is it?" Fred asked with genuine concern. Lillian blinked and slightly turned toward Fred without making eye contact. She didn't speak for several seconds.

"I didn't go to work today because I got fired," she finally said.

"Why?" Fred asked. He held his breath in anticipation of the response.

"Well, you know I hand out perfume samples at the department store, right?

"Uh-huh," Fred responded. *Don't tell me she stole some perfume*, he thought.

His palms began to sweat as he thought about the samples he had taken the liberty of keeping for himself when he had been instructed to destroy and throw them away. *If my boss found out, I could be fired too*, Fred thought.

The idea of having to return to Norfolk and stay under Hun Taylor's roof again caused Fred's temperature to rise. He loosened his collar and swallowed hard.

"Some of the customers don't want to take the perfume samples from a colored girl," Lillian said.

"What?" Fred asked perplexed. He was so caught up in his own thoughts that he didn't hear Lillian.

"I said they fired me because some of the customers didn't want to take the perfume samples from a colored girl," Lillian repeated, but the last line was in a higher octave.

"Aw, Babby, I'm so sorry to hear that. Those fool white ladies should be honored to have a beautiful colored girl try to help them improve their look or smell or whatever," Fred said in an attempt to cheer her up. Lillian gave Fred a half smile and then placed her chin on his shoulder.

"I really needed that job," Lillian sighed. "I help support my parents. My daddy got hurt working at the lumberyard. Now he can only get odd-job work here and there. They don't pay much. And my mom," Lillian paused, "well she can't work."

"Why, did she get hurt on the job too," Fred asked sincerely.

"No, she just ain't right in the head," Lillian confided. "My daddy takes care of her the best he can, and I help out by bringing home some extra money."

Fred wondered what she meant when she said that her mother wasn't right in the head. For a moment he felt a pang of nervous jitters in his gut, however, he quickly decided to shake off the feeling.

"Don't worry Lillian, I'll ask my boss if he can use a pretty, smart girl like you at the drugstore," Fred said patting her on the back.

Lillian's eyes lit up. "Oh Fred, do you think he will hire me?"

"I can't make any promises, but it can't hurt to ask," Fred said.

"Thank you, Fred," Lillian said.

The look of relief on her face made Fred feel good about himself. He felt like the hero in the comic books, who swooped down and saved the damsel in distress. His self-imposed hero status was solidified when his boss hired Lillian part time taking orders at the lunch counter.

* * *

"You're not eating lunch again?" Fred asked Lillian.

"No, I'm not really that hungry," Lillian said sighing.

The two strolled side by side. Fred held a ham sandwich wrapped in wax paper in one hand and Lillian's hand in the other. When they reached the park, they chose their usual bench under an oak tree. Lillian sat with her legs crossed at the ankles. She ran her hands down her skirt in a brisk motion like she was brushing something off. She gazed across the park and locked eyes on a weeping willow tree. She held her gaze there for several minutes without blinking until the sound of Fred's voice brought her out of her trance.

"You okay?" Fred asked. Lillian nodded but didn't speak.

"Here, eat half of this sandwich. You look like you're wasting away."

"I said I'm not hungry," Lillian said in a curt tone. She folded her arms and stiffened her body, keeping her eyes fixed on the willow tree. Fred hunched his shoulders.

"Suit yourself," Fred said in a miffed tone.

He leaned back on the park bench and crossed his legs, ankle to knee. He took a bite from his sandwich. During the past months of taking orders at the lunch counter, Fred had noticed that Lillian ate very little. He had thought this was odd behavior but had surmised that maybe she was just a finicky eater.

He then recalled her statement about her mother not being right in the head when they first had lunch together. Not wanting to make much of it, he justified it in his mind that perhaps her mother had become old and ditzy like his Grandmother Fannie had started to become. Dora had brought Fannie to Norfolk for that very reason.

"Penny for your thoughts," Lillian said, startling Fred.

"What?" Fred stammered.

"It's time to get back," Lillian said pointing to her watch.

She hopped up from the bench and grabbed the wax paper wrapper from Fred's hand. He watched her as she skipped over to the trash can to discard the wrapper. Lillian ran back to the bench where Fred was still sitting. She grabbed his hand and tugged.

"Come one, let's go," she said giggling.

Fred gave a half smile and rose from the bench. They walked back to the store hand in hand. Lillian occasionally swung their clasped hands back and forth like a playful child. For a moment, Fred looked at Lillian with his brow wrinkled. He was perplexed by her buoyant disposition when she was so sullen just moments ago. He quickly softened his facial expression when she looked up smiling at him.

"Well, I'm glad to see you're in a better mood," he said.

"What do you mean by that?" Lillian asked curtly. Her demeanor had once again changed. She unclasped her hand from his and ran the rest of the way back to the store.

"Lillian," Fred called out. "Wait a minute."

But she did not stop.

She's acting like that Jekyll and Hyde from the movie, Fred thought.

When he finally arrived at the store, Lillian was busy wiping the countertop. He decided to go back to his room. He figured he could find out what was going on with Lillian later.

Chapter 23

The beginning of 1939 offered new hope and opportunity for Fred and Lillian. Their whirlwind courtship culminated into Lillian moving into Fred's room over the store. The situation was not ideal. As much as Fred liked having her around, he equally disliked sharing the cramped quarters. But his discomfort wouldn't last for long.

"Fred, can you come see me for a moment?" Fred's boss called out from his office.

"Yes, sir." Fred set down the box he was carrying.

"Shut the door," his boss instructed when Fred entered the office.

Fred stood in front of his boss's desk with his hands clasped in front of him. He felt nervous. Thoughts raced through his head, and the quivering he felt in the pit of his stomach intensified. Fred searched his memory trying to figure out why he was being called into the office.

What could I have done wrong? He asked himself. *Is it my relationship with Lillian?* He wondered. *The fact that she's staying with me now in my room?*

Beads of sweat formed on his forehead. He reached in his pocket and pulled out a square, white linen handkerchief. After wiping his brow, he cleared his throat.

"Er, is there something wrong, sir?" Fred asked. He considered himself lucky to be steadily employed during a decade that was in such an economic slump. He wondered if his luck had finally run out.

"No, Fred. Everything is fine," his boss responded, interrupting Fred's thoughts. "The manager over at the Standard Drug on West Cary has a porter position open. He asked me if I had anyone that can fill the position. I thought of you."

"Me, sir?" Fred questioned. Fred didn't seem to recognize his own potential.

"Yes. I told the manager, Mr. Stewart, that you've been working the first shift here for over a year. You've been doing a fine job, but frankly, I'm going to have to cut the first shift's hours in half. That would be a cut in pay for you. Over at Stewart's store, the hours would be from eight in the morning to four in the afternoon, and the pay is a buck and a quarter more than you make here."

Fred stood as straight as an arrow. His body was tense, and his breathing was shallow. He had anticipated bad news, not the beginning of something wonderful.

"More money," Fred stammered.

"Yep," his boss said, smiling.

"Thank you, sir, but," Fred hesitated.

"But what?"

"Er, I was wondering if Mr. Stewart's store had living quarters like here."

Fred's boss chuckled. "No, sorry Fred, no such luck. This here is a unique situation, but I'll tell you what I'm going to do."

"What's that?"

"I'm going to ask Mr. Stewart to recommend a place that you can afford to rent. How does that sound?"

"That sounds great sir. When do I start?"

"In two weeks."

* * *

"Oh, Fred, it's lovely," Lillian said, gushing over the one-bedroom rental she and Fred would be sharing on Rose Avenue. Lillian thought that the antique-white painted walls could have used a coat of fresh paint, but she didn't mind.

The apartment was furnished with a slightly worn navy-blue sofa adorned with two square blue and white checkerboard-patterned throw pillows. The sofa was positioned in front of a casement window dressed with panel curtains that matched the sofa pillows. A breakfast nook counter divided the living room from the kitchen and was equipped with two wooden stools.

Lillian walked across the room to the bedroom door. When she looked inside the room, she was a bit disappointed. The small bedroom only held a double bed pushed flush against the wall and a four-drawer chest. She crinkled her nose in an expression of discontentment.

"Huh, it's a little tight in there," she said looking over her shoulder at Fred who was standing directly behind her. Fred nodded in acknowledgement but didn't speak.

"Let's see the bathroom," Lillian said gently pushing Fred to the side. When she opened the bathroom room door her eyes widened. She drew her hand up to her chest.

"Oh my goodness," she exclaimed.

"What is it?" Fred asked coming up behind her.

"It's a claw-footed bathtub," she said, gawking.

"That's some fancy shit," Fred said.

The tub was old and in need of a thorough cleaning, but Lillian was unfazed. She was up to the challenge of making this antique tub the pride of their apartment.

"I can't wait to soak in this tub. It's fit for a queen," Lillian said dreamy eyed.

Fred looked at her adoringly and once again felt like a superhero. He had made her dreams come true without even trying. She was happy, and he thought that through her eyes he could do anything. Fred placed his hands on Lillian's shoulders as she continued to gaze at the tub. She reached up and placed her hands on top of his and gently exhaled.

"You know," Fred said in a voice just above a whisper, "we should make this living arrangement official."

Lillian's eye's widened. She whipped around to face Fred. "What do you mean?" Lillian slightly trembled.

"I mean we should get married," Fred responded matter-of-factly.

Lillian cupped her hand over her mouth as tears formed in her eyes.

"Really Fred?" She managed to ask.

"Yes," he said softly.

Lillian blinked and a single tear rolled down her cheek.

* * *

By the summer of 1940, Fred and Lillian were married. Fred had taken a job as a stock clerk at the Richmond Fruit Company on Cary Street. His new boss, Frank Burton, paid only a quarter more an hour than Mr. Stewart, but Fred needed to make more money to support his wife. She hadn't worked since leaving her job taking orders at Standard Drug where she and Fred had met.

Now she spent her days keeping the apartment clean, washing and ironing clothes, and at the end of the day, taking a long relaxing bath in her claw-footed tub. On Sundays, she attended the Church of Christ on North Avenue, just blocks away from their apartment. She had gotten Fred to attend church with her once, but he had little patience for how long the service had lasted. One Sunday after church, Lillian entered the apartment with some exciting news.

"Hey, Fred, guess what?"

"I don't know. What?" Fred responded sitting on the sofa drinking a beer and listening to a baseball game on the radio.

"It's Sunday for Christ's sake," Lillian scolded when she saw the beer can.

"Is that your big news?" Fred replied sarcastically while turning the can up to his lips.

Lillian sucked in a breath and rolled her eyes. "It's the Lord's Day, Fred. Can't you lay off the beer for one day?" she disparaged.

She removed her white gloves and white Kentucky Derby styled hat.

"Anyway, my news is that the pastor and his wife asked me to babysit their two little boys twice a week while they do missionary work."

"What kind of missionary work are they doing?" Fred asked, cutting his eyes and scowling at his wife.

"They mostly visit and minister to people in hospitals, nursing homes, and the elderly members of the church. They read the scriptures, sing songs, and pray with them. Stuff like that. Pastor's wife said she sure missed doing missionary work with her husband since having the boys."

"So they asked you to watch their boys—you out of all the people in that church—over people that they have known far longer than you?" Fred asked.

"What are you trying to say?" Lillian asked. She plopped down on the sofa next to her husband.

"I just think they are taking advantage of you because you're new there," Fred snapped, throwing his head back to down the last swig of beer.

"It's not like that, Fred. Besides, I'm not doing it for free. They offered to pay me two dollars," Lillian beamed.

Fred didn't reply. He turned his attention back to the ball game on the radio. Lillian let out a heavy sigh expressing her displeasure with Fred's dismissiveness of her.

"Well, I'll let you get back to your game," she said, tapping him on the thigh. She rose and went into the bedroom.

* * *

Lillian sat on the burgundy winged chair reading the book of Psalms in the pastor and his wife's living room. The couple had left just thirty minutes earlier, and the boys were already fast asleep in their bedroom. As she turned a page in her Bible, she was startled by a key turning in the door. When the door swung open, Lillian jumped to her feet, causing the Bible in her lap to fall to the floor.

"Pastor, you scared me," Lillian said breathlessly. She could feel the pulse of her heartbeat pounding at the base of her neck. "Why are you back so soon," she asked, her voice cracking.

The pastor did not respond. He gently closed the door and moved toward Lillian.

"Where is your wife?" She asked, craning her neck in an attempt to see behind him.

He placed his finger to his lips in a gesture for her to stop speaking.

"It's just the two of us," he whispered. "My wife is at the nursing home this evening. I told her that I had to take care of some business at the church and would be back for her later."

"So why are you here?" Lillian asked. The question was rhetorical. The look of lust in his eyes told her all she needed to know. She moved behind the winged chair.

"Oh, come now, pretty lady," the pastor jeered. "You worldly women understand the needs of the flesh. This can be our little secret. My wife and your husband don't have to know."

Lillian stood rigid, holding onto the back of the chair. She cocked her head and narrowed her eyes.

What did he just call me?

She paused for a moment to gather her thoughts. She needed a moment to process what was happening. She had been deceived by a man of the cloth. Fred's insinuation about the reason she was picked to babysit came flooding back to her memory.

"So they asked you to watch their boys—you out of all the people in that church that they have known far longer than you." She remembered Fred saying this. Lillian felt like a fool. How could she be so gullible? Ambivalence settled into her spirit. She felt both sadness and anger at the same time. But soon, anger won out.

"Why you dirty bastard," Lillian said glaring up at the pastor with eyes as red as fire.

The pastor's eyes bucked in disbelief. "What did you say?" He asked as if he was shocked by her reaction.

"Don't you even think about putting your filthy hands on me," Lillian said in a low, gravelly voice.

She moved slowly around the wing chair with her eyes still fixed on the pastor. He stood motionless as if entranced by her glare. His eyes followed her as she walked over to the sofa to retrieve her purse. Lillian backed her way to the door never breaking eye contact with the pastor, who stood as still as a statue. When she finally reached the door, she flung it open and ran out of the house all the way home. Fred was reaching for a beer in the refrigerator when Lillian burst through the front door.

"What the hell?" Fred asked.

"You were right, Fred. That dirty dog made a pass at me," Lillian blurted out. "He left his wife at the nursing home and made up a lie about having to go back to the church for something. But instead he came back to the house. I'm not going back to that church."

"Damn right you're not going back," Fred said.

Lillian ran into Fred's arms. They embraced. Fred had to ask the question that he dreaded, but needed to know.

"Did he touch you?" Fred whispered.

Lillian squeezed Fred tightly around the waist. "No, I told that filthy bastard that he'd better not lay a finger on me."

Fred gave Lillian a gentle kiss on the forehead. "Why don't you go run yourself a bath? You'll feel better," he said.

"Good idea." Lillian went into the bathroom and shut the door.

When Fred heard the water in the tub running, he took his beer and plopped down on the sofa. He was both angered and disenchanted by the hypocrisy of a trusted member of society.

You don't expect a so-called man of God to be a masher, and you certainly don't expect him to deny his own family members, Fred thought, now remembering Reverend Frink.

Fred and Lillian never spoke of the incident again. But afterward, Fred was put off by all ministers. He figured that these men used the Bible and their robes to disguise that they were really wolves in sheep's clothing.

Fred also began to come to the realization that he didn't have what it took to be Lillian's hero. In a way, Fred too wore a disguise—the mask that portrayed him as Lillian's protector. But in reality, Fred knew that he didn't have the courage or the confidence to confront the pastor about the incident, which left him feeling emasculated.

Lillian hadn't asked him to confront the minister. And secretly, Fred was relieved that she hadn't. He wondered if on some level she knew that he was incapable of confrontation and that he really wasn't a superhero. Feeling inadequate after work the following night, instead of purchasing a six-pack of beer, Fred bought a pint of gin.

Chapter 24

Fred stumbled into his apartment at a quarter to midnight on a Friday night with the bib of his cap cocked to one side. His shirttail was untucked, and his pants were twisted to the side in a poor attempt to conceal a urine stain. The stench of gin and tobacco engulfed him, but Fred was oblivious. He weaved his way across the room to the kitchen area and opened the refrigerator door.

"Huh, she didn't cook nothing again for dinner," Fred mumbled, head halfway in. He slammed the door and looked up at the cupboard. *Let's see what we got up here*, he thought, reaching for the door but losing his balance in the process.

Fred hit the floor hard. He landed on his left side, and the force of the fall caused the dishes on the counter to rattle. Fred lay there for several seconds, with his arm straight over his head, and stared at the floor. He rolled onto his stomach and got on his hands and knees. With his right hand, he reached up and grabbed the counter in an attempt to hoist himself back up. On the way up, his hand slipped and he fell again, this time falling on his right side.

Undeterred, Fred positioned himself so that his back was flushed against the lower kitchen cabinets for balance. He placed his feet flat on the floor and used his hands to lift himself off the floor. Once he was on his feet, he started to feel dizzy. He covered his eyes. It felt like the room was spinning. Once it stopped, Fred looked in the top cabinet for something to eat. His eyes widened when he found a box of saltine crackers and a can of sardines.

That's the ticket, he whispered.

Fred sat at the kitchen counter with his elbows on the table and one hand cupped under his chin. He had taken a bite of the cracker with a single sardine lying on top. His eyes were closed, and he chewed so long and so slowly that the contents in his mouth liquefied. He took another bite. The crunching sound in his ears muffled what he thought was the sound of someone whispering. Fred opened his eyes and swallowed hard.

He walked over to the bedroom door and opened it just enough to stick his head inside. The room was dark and quiet. Fred looked at the bed and squinted. He couldn't tell if the lump on the bed was pillows or Lillian. He opened the door fully to allow the light from the living room area to shine through. Fred saw that the room was empty. He frowned.

Where could she be? He stood in the doorway for several seconds when he heard the whispers again. He cocked his head and realized the sound was coming from the bathroom. Fred turned slowly and walked to the bathroom door. He gently knocked.

"Psst, Lillian. You in there?" Fred asked through the closed door.

The whispering stopped, but Fred didn't receive a response. He knocked again, this time a little harder; but again got no response. Fred grabbed the knob and opened the door. His eyes narrowed at the sight of Lillian sitting in the claw-footed tub fully clothed. She was rocking back and forth. She was whispering an unintelligible mixture of random words and phrases.

Is she speaking in tongues or something? Fred thought in his drunken state.

Whatever was going on with her Fred didn't want to deal with it. He shrugged his shoulders and chose to ignore her strange behavior. He closed the bathroom door and walked over to the sofa and sat down. He closed his eyes and fell asleep sitting up.

Fred, still on the sofa, awoke to the warmth of the sun shining through the living room window. He glanced down at his watch. It was 9 a.m. He looked over and saw that the bathroom door was open and the bedroom door was closed.

Lillian must be in the bedroom now, Fred thought.

Now he wondered if the sight of his fully clothed wife rocking back and forth in the claw-footed tub had just been a figment of his inebriated imagination. He arose from the sofa but quickly sat back down.

"Whoa," He said, holding his head.

He felt dizzy. He got up again and staggered over to the breakfast nook. His half-eaten saltine crackers and sardines were strewn there. Fred polished off the food and got up to peek in on Lillian. When he reached the door, he saw that she was still fully clothed, lying diagonally across the bed, and fast asleep. Fred held his throbbing head and made his way back to the sofa. He lay there and drifted back to sleep.

* * *

In the summer of 1942, the lease on Fred and Lillian's Rose Avenue apartment expired. The rent was going up, and Fred's salary had not increased enough to cover it. He found another apartment they could afford about two miles away on Hunt Avenue.

The next change Fred would make was with his job. He had grown weary of all the heavy lifting as a stock clerk at Virginia Food. He was able to score a checkout clerk position at the Royal Club Food Store, just a block away from Virginia Food. His new boss, Mr. Crowe, would be the first black man Fred ever worked for. Although Fred was pleased with these changes, Lillian was not.

"But I don't want to move," Lillian screamed like a banshee. She sat in the middle of the bed with her legs crisscrossed. "I don't want to leave my claw-footed tub," she screeched, shaking her head frantically.

Fred stood at the bedroom door with his hands in his pockets. "Calm down, Babby," he said after taking a deep breath.

Fred had long since given up trying to be Lillian's hero. He had also grown weary of her adolescent-like fits. All he could do was try to keep a roof over their heads and food in the cupboard.

"It can't be helped, dear," Fred tried to say in a calm even tone. "I'm the only one working here."

"Oh, there you go. I was wondering when you was going to start in on me about not working," Lillian shouted.

"I didn't say anything about you not working. I'm just saying that I had to find a place that I can afford," Fred said exasperated.

It was true that Lillian couldn't seem to hold onto a job for more than three months.

It's always something, Fred thought. *To let her tell it, her coworkers are either spying on her, talking about her behind her back, or trying to get her fired, so she quits.* Fred now began to think that she wasn't fired from her job at the department store handing out perfume samples but had quit.

"I don't want to leave my tub," Lillian said, interrupting Fred's thoughts. Her voice was now childlike. She stared at the bed and twirled her hair through her fingers.

"Well, we can't take it with us," Fred said.

"I know," Lillian replied still speaking in her childlike voice.

Fred shook his head and decided to try to change the subject. "Listen, I'm getting a little wolfie. Why don't you get dressed, and we can go down to the wharf and get some seafood," Fred suggested.

Lillian switched from childlike mode back to banshee mode. "I don't want to eat. You can't make me eat," Lillian shouted. She threw herself on her back and covered her face with a pillow.

Fred rolled his eyes upward, sucked his teeth, and then existed the room.

I can't stand this shit, he thought. Fred believed Lillian's outrageous behavior was an attempt to manipulate him. He found that the best way to deal with her was not to deal with her at all. He avoided her as much as he could.

I wish I could get away from here for a while, Fred thought. In the coming months, his wish would regrettably come true. On December 7, 1942, on the one-year anniversary of the attack on Pearl Harbor, Fred received a cablegram informing him of the death of his beloved grandmother, Fannie Smith.

* * *

The two-hour Greyhound bus ride from Richmond back to Norfolk gave Fred time to reminisce about Fannie. He had fond memories of the two of them eating stage planks and cheese on those nights when she had worked late and had been too tired to cook. And when he had had an especially hard day after school and the older boys had taunted him, she had made his favorite supper.

"How bout I make you some Hoppin' John and corn bread," Fred thought he heard Fannie whispering in his ear. He flinched and put his hand up to his ear. A single tear trickled down his cheek.

"I'm gonna miss you Momma Fannie," Fred whispered, wiping his face.

"There he is," Fred heard a young man yelling in his direction. "Fred," the young man yelled, now waving his arms in the air. "It's me, Jimmy." Fred's eyes widened.

"Oh my God," Fred exclaimed walking toward Jimmy. "Boy, I haven't seen you in a coon's age." The two hugged and slapped each other on the back.

"How's Momma holding up without Momma Fannie?" Fred asked.

"She's holding up okay, I guess. Them two was thick as thieves, you know," Jimmy said.

"Yes, I know."

"Well, come on. I got the old man's car. Let me get you back to the house."

"Has my aunt Dee-Dee arrived yet?"

"She wasn't there when I left, but her and her husband supposed to get here sometime today. But they're not staying at the house. They're getting a hotel."

"A hotel? Why is that?" Fred asked. Jimmy snickered.

"Well, your auntie really ain't too keen on Hun." Fred rolled his eyes toward the sky. He could relate. "She got mad at him," Jimmy continued.

"Why, what did he do?" Fred asked.

"Well, we was all up in New York for a visit. By the way, she got a fine house. Anyway, while she was out of the room, Hun turned on her phonograph. Momma told him to leave it alone. He didn't even know what the damn thing was anyway."

"Don't tell me he broke it," Fred asked interrupting.

"Naw, but he might as well have," Jimmy continued.

"Why is that?"

"Well he had turned the damn thing on but didn't know it. We all went out to dinner and when we came back, you could smell the heat from this thing."

Fred looked puzzled. "Smell the heat, what do you mean?"

"I don't know. Your aunt Dee-Dee explained it, but I can't remember. All I know is that she was pissed at Hun. I heard her call him an ignorant bastard under her breath."

Fred threw his head back and laughed. "Yep, he sure is."

When Jimmy parked the car in front of his mother's house on O'Keefe Street, a feeling of ambivalence surrounded Fred. He was excited to see his mother and aunt again, but knowing that he would never see his grandmother alive again, caused Fred great pain. When Jimmy and Fred entered the house, the first person they saw was Hun. He was sitting on the sofa.

"Look who's here," Jimmy announced in a loud voice.

Dora ran into the living room from the kitchen, wiping her hands on her apron. "Freddie," she screamed.

They hugged for several seconds. When they finally released their embrace, Fred gasped when he saw his Aunt Alethia standing directly behind his mother.

"Aunt Dee-Dee," Fred exclaimed.

"Fred," his aunt said with outstretched arms. The two hugged while rocking slightly from right to left.

"Let me look at you," Alethia finally said after their long embrace. She stepped back a bit and looked Fred up and down. She beamed. "You're all grown up now," she said looking up at him with moist eyes.

"Yes, I'm twenty-nine years old," Fred said, laughing.

"And you're taller than me."

Everyone in the room laughed except Hun. Fred sensed the imbalance in the room and cut his eyes over in his stepfather's direction.

"Hi, Hun," Fred said.

Hun looked over in Fred's direction. "Fred," Hun said nodding his head.

With the awkward formalities out the way, Fred returned his attention to his mother and aunt. "So Momma, what happened? Was Grand Momma sick?" Fred asked.

"No, son. She just passed quietly in her sleep. She's at Hale's Funeral Home now. She's going to be buried at West Point Cemetery," Dora said. She took Fred by the hand and led him into the kitchen. "Come on in the kitchen, you must be hungry," Dora said. Alethia followed close behind.

* * *

Fannie's service was held on Saturday. After the funeral, Fred did not want to return to Dora and Hun's for the repast. The idea of all those church folks at the house caused him to feel anxious. He was not comfortable in most social situations, but he had a particular aversion to the religious community. He sat next to Jimmy on the ride home from the cemetery. He leaned over to speak to him.

"Listen, can we go somewhere else besides back to Momma's," Fred whispered to Jimmy with his mouth turned slightly.

"What do you have in mind?" Jimmy asked in an equally low tone.

"How about a bar?"

"Well, I'm not old enough to go to a bar," Jimmy chuckled, "but I know someplace just as good."

"Where?"

"Over on Lexington, my buddy Bobby's big brother sells liquor in his house."

Fred nodded and gave Jimmy a wink. When they arrived back at Dora and Hun's house, the family filed out of the black limousine. Once they were on the sidewalk, Jimmy pulled Dora to the side.

"Momma, listen. Me and Fred don't want to be around a bunch of old church folks."

"Jimmy," Dora said frowning.

"Momma, I don't mean no disrespect," he said with his arm around her shoulders. "I'm just going to take Fred over to my friend's place for a while."

Dora gave him a disapproving look. Jimmy smiled and gave her a light kiss on the forehead. Dora's face softened.

"Well, just stay out of trouble," Dora said tapping Jimmy affectionately on the arm. Fred and Jimmy walked down O'Keefe and made a right onto Lexington Street. It was a brisk winter day but not bitterly cold. The collars on their coats were turned up, and their hands were in their pockets. They walked in silence until Fred decided to make small talk.

"So Jim, this is your last year at Booker T?" Fred asked.

"Yep," Jimmy said.

"What are your plans after graduation?"

"I'm joining the navy," Jimmy said proudly.

"Really? You're only seventeen. Is Hun going to sign for you?"

"He won't have to sign for me. I'll be eighteen this February, and the recruiter said I can ship out right after graduation in May."

"Why do you want to join the navy?" Fred questioned.

"Hey, man, anything to get out of Norfolk, right? You left."

"Yeah, but it was more about getting out from under Hun's thumb."

"I hear you. I'm looking at it like this: I get three meals a day, a roof over my head, money in my pocket, and clothes on my back, all courtesy of Uncle Sam. I'll take that deal all day long."

As the two men stepped onto the porch of Jimmy's friend, Fred thought Jimmy's plan was a stroke of genius.

"Say, Jim," Fred said, grabbing Jimmy's wrist to prevent him from knocking on his friend's front door.

"What is it?" Jimmy replied.

"What's the age limit on getting into the military?"

"I don't know about other branches but it's thirty-four if you're thinking about the navy."

"I'm actually thinking about the army," Fred said with a smirk on his face. "You actually make a good case for joining up."

"And the recruiter told me that I can set up a monthly allotment to send Momma money. You could do that for your wife," Jimmy added.

"I could indeed," Fred mumbled.

* * *

Fred returned to Richmond feeling a sense of dread. He didn't know what type of mood his wife would be in, and he had gotten good at avoiding her as much as possible. He'd gotten in the habit of frequenting the local bar after work to numb his angst.

His little brother had given him an idea of how to escape Richmond, and he was fascinated about the possibility, so much so, that he stopped by the local recruiting office before going home. The recruiter told him that if he passed the physical examination, he could be on his way to basic training in less than two months.

When Fred entered their new apartment, he was surprised to see Lillian on her knees in the bathroom scrubbing the tub.

"Hi, Lily. I'm back," he said standing in the bathroom doorway.

Lillian stood and turned her body in Fred's direction. The sun peeking through the bathroom curtains gave the appearance of a halo over Lillian's head. To Fred, her face appeared to glow. She had a smile on her face, and this put Fred at ease.

"Fred," she exclaimed, "I'm so glad you're back."

Lillian walked over to him. She stood on her toes, craned her neck forward, and puckered her lips. Fred bent down and gave his wife a gentle kiss.

"Hey, Babby, when you get done in here, come to the living room. I have something I want to talk to you about."

"Okay," Lillian said smiling.

She returned to her spot on the floor in front of the tub. Fred went into the kitchen and retrieved a beer from the refrigerator. Sitting on the sofa, he patiently waited for Lillian to finish up in the bathroom. With each sip of beer, Fred pondered how he would broach the subject of joining the army with her.

After twenty minutes, Lillian finally emerged from the bathroom. She walked over to the refrigerator and pulled out a cold soda. When she popped the can, foam rose to the top and spilled out. She quickly cupped her mouth over the can opening and giggled. Lillian plopped down on the sofa next to Fred and a heavy sigh escaped her.

"So, what is it that you wanted to talk about?" Lillian asked, taking a sip of her soda.

"Er, you know how hard it's been for me to earn a decent amount of money."

"Oh, hell, is this about me getting a job again?" Lillian interrupted. "Fred I told you—"

"No that's not what this is about," Fred interjected. "I was thinking that the best way for me to earn good money is to join the army.

"The army," Lillian screamed.

"Just hear me out," Fred said trying to keep her calm. "If I join the service that would mean a steady paycheck, more money, and medical and dental care. Babby, it would mean I could give you the life you deserve. You wouldn't want for nothing."

Fred knew he was laying it on thick, but he had to convince Lillian that this was a good idea. He had to sell her on how much she would benefit so she would buy into the plan. Lillian sat next to Fred as still as a statue. She looked straight ahead and didn't speak for several seconds. She finally blinked and then turned to look at Fred.

"I don't want you to go," Lillian finally said. "It's a war going on. You can't fight. You will be killed."

"Aw, Babby, you can't think like that. First of all, I will learn everything I need to know at basic training. Besides, I'm not going to be on the front lines in combat. The recruiter said I would either be serving food in the mess hall or issuing gear."

"I can't live alone, Fred," Lillian said with sad eyes.

"You don't have to live alone. You can move back with your folks while I'm away. The money I'll be sending will help them too. You can go back to helping them like you were when we first met."

Lillian smiled at this. "I did feel proud to be helping my parents." Lillian placed her chin on Fred's shoulder. "So how long would you have to serve?"

"About two and a half years." Lillian's head popped up.

"Two and a half years," she exclaimed. "My God, Fred, that's an eternity."

"I'll be able to come home to visit," Fred said, lying.

Lillian placed her head back on Fred's shoulder and let out a sigh as if trying to resign herself to the notion that her husband would be leaving but doing it in order to take care of her. She seemed to take comfort in that knowledge.

* * *

In July 1943, Fred enlisted into the United States Army. He traveled to a recruiting office in Virginia Beach to meet the army bus that would transport him and thirty other recruits to Fort Dix in New Jersey, for basic training.

The physical training for the twenty-nine-year-old Fred was a challenge in the beginning. He was no longer the swift gazelle he once was when running from bullies, but he kept pace with the younger men in his squad. He found the calisthenics challenging at first, but soon mastered the variety of motor movements. It was the push-ups that proved most difficult for Fred. If he wasn't able to complete the required amount of correct push-ups, he would not pass the military physical fitness test.

"Damn it, Private Smith. I want to see your chest hit that ground," his drill sergeant would yell at him every time he caught Fred doing an incorrect push-up.

"Yes, drill sergeant," Fred would scream through his pain.

After successfully completing his basic training in August 1943, Fred began to work on the base as a supply clerk. Throughout basic training, he wrote to Lillian, who was living with her parents, every week. Her replies to him were sporadic at best, but by November, he had not received one reply to his letters. One day, the first sergeant called him into his office.

"At ease soldier," the first sergeant said.

Fred got into position by standing with his feet shoulder width apart and his hands clasped behind his back.

"Your father-in-law contacted the Red Cross about your wife."

Fred's heart sank. He couldn't imagine what the news could be. He stiffened his back and braced himself.

"It appears your wife has had some type of psychotic episode. Her father said she claims to hear voices and sounds that nobody else hears and sees things that are not there."

Memories in Fred's mind flipped like pages in a book. He recalled the night he had found Lillian sitting fully clothed in the claw-footed tub at the apartment on Rose Avenue. He had been drunk that night and had chosen to ignore what was apparently a strange occurrence. He had remembered her mood swings and had elected to justify them as her trying to manipulate him in order to get her way.

"The last straw was when she took a knife to her father," the first sergeant said interrupting Fred's thoughts.

"Sir?" Fred said in a questioning tone.

"They said she took a knife to her father. She thought he was a giant snake."

"Where is she now?" Fred spoke in a voice just above a whisper.

"She's in the local hospital right now, but you're going to have to go back to sign her into a mental hospital."

Fred's head was spinning. He felt like he would pass out.

"Private Smith, did you hear me?" Fred refocused his attention on the first sergeant, who was holding out a sheet of paper.

"No, sorry, sergeant."

"I said I'm giving you a thirty-day pass to return home to take care of your wife. You leave at 0800 tomorrow."

Fred arrived in Richmond at 12:30 p.m. His body was stiff after the four and a half hour bus ride. He walked around to the window at the back of the bus terminal where colored people could order food. After waiting nearly thirty minutes for the cook to finish waiting on all the white customers, Fred was finally able to order a sandwich and a soft drink. He sat on the wooden bench, which was positioned adjacent to the window and ate his lunch. While eating, he remembered the first time he and Lillian had had lunch together in the park.

When Fred finally arrived at Lillian's parents' house, her father, Mr. Corbin, greeted him. On the way to the hospital, Mr. Corbin revealed to Fred that Lillian had not had such a violent episode since she was nineteen.

Fred's face flushed. It felt like heat was rising from the pit of his stomach. *Lillian has been sick all this time and no one bothered to tell me*, Fred thought.

A flood of emotions surged over Fred—first fear and then anger. But when he arrived at the hospital and saw his wife in a straightjacket, the emotion that replaced the others was shame. This feeling had followed him his whole life. His grandfather, who was a minister, was ashamed to have a grandson who was born out of wedlock. He passed that shame onto his son George, who was ashamed to publically acknowledge Fred. His grandmother had pretended to be his mother, and his mother had pretended to be his sister in order to cover the shame. Now Fred found out that he had a mentally ill wife. He simply couldn't bear any more shame. He wanted to hide it, run away from it, and not look back.

"What do I have to sign?" Fred asked.

"I'll get the doctor to bring you the transfer forms," the nurse in the room said.

The following morning Lillian was transported to the Central Lunatic Asylum in Petersburg, Virginia, where she remained for the rest of her life.

Chapter 25

SOUTHPORT, NORTH CAROLINA

December 1912

Dora stood at the kitchen sink, tears flowing. The more she wiped, the more they flowed. Before long, she was on her knees openly sobbing. Hearing her sobs from the bedroom they shared, her eleven-year-old sister, Alethia, leapt from her bed and ran into the kitchen.

"What's wrong Doe?" Alethia said, nearly in tears herself as she witnessed her big sister's obvious pain.

Dora did not answer, she couldn't control her sobbing. A burden of guilt weighed heavily on her for several weeks, and now the flood gates were opened.

"Momma, Poppa," Alethia called out to her parents. "Something's happened to Doe." She feverishly knocked on her parents' bedroom door. Their father, Romeo, jumped from his bed wearing his nightshirt and quickly followed his younger daughter into the kitchen. Their mother, Fannie, soon followed, tying the sash of her robe.

"What is it, child?" Fannie asked.

Dora's sobbing had ceased but she could not bear to look up at her family, who had gathered in a half circle around her. Sitting on the floor with her face toward her lap and her head in her hands, Dora mumbled, "I'm so ashamed. Momma, Poppa, I am so sorry."

"Tell us what happened, Dora," said her father in a booming but gentle voice.

Dora was a daddy's girl. While growing up, she had been particularly attached to her father. He had indulged her and would do pretty much anything for her. To him, she could do no wrong. Dora feared that her father would no longer feel the same after she told him what she had done.

Fannie sat on the floor and cradled her daughter in her arms. Fearing the worst possible news, she braced herself. "Go on, chil'. Just tell it to us straight."

Dora looked into her mother's tear-filled eyes. "I'm pregnant," she whispered.

Fannie closed her eyes and tightened her grip on Dora. "You sure, chil'?" Fannie asked rocking her daughter. "You miss your time?"

"Yes ma'am," Dora answered in a flat tone.

"Who's the poppa?"

"George Frink."

"Oh Lord, have mercy. Not Reverend Frink's boy," Fannie exclaimed.

"Damn it. I can't believe this," Dora heard her father say as he walked back to his bedroom and slammed the door behind him.

Dora closed her eyes and attempted to block out the world outside their door. As her mother continued to gently rock her, Dora's mind drifted back to that horrific summer day, just weeks ago, when a local fisherman, Tom Moore, had burst into the press shop where her mother worked.

"Miss Fannie, Miss Fannie." Dora remembered Tom Moore's frantic screams as he had entered the shop soaking wet.

"What is it, Mr. Moore?" Fannie responded. "What happened

to you? Why are you all wet?" Fannie had braced herself for bad news.

Dora and Alethia had both been at the shop that day helping Fannie press shirts. They had hurried to their mother's side to hear what the hysterical Mr. Moore had come to tell them.

"It's your boy, Wilbur, Miss Fannie. He drowned in the river. Me and my buddy Bobby saw him and jumped in to try to save him, but the currents were too rough. We couldn't reach him in time."

"Oh my God, no. No, please God, no," Fannie screamed as she started sobbing and dropped to her knees. "My boy, my boy, oh Lord, oh Lord," she cried.

"Miss Fannie, I'm so, so sorry," Tom said trying to console her.

"Where's my boy? I want to see him," Fannie continued in agony.

Dora and Alethia had joined their mother on the floor. With a daughter on each side, they put their arms around Fannie and cried with her.

"Bobby went to get your husband, Miss Fannie. They're going back to the riverbank to look for Wilbur," Tom said.

The search for Wilbur had gone on for several hours, but his body had not been recovered. A memorial service had been held at the Mount Zion Baptist Church two weeks after the tragic accident.

The family mourned their loss separately, not speaking of it among themselves. Romeo drank more to numb his pain while Fannie worked later hours at the press shop. Alethia spent all her time with her nose in some sort of book. Dora stayed busy with housekeeping and cooking the family meals. The tranquil life of the Smith family had changed for the worse the day Wilbur died, but the winds of change for the family had only just begun to blow.

That's when all our lives took a nose dive, Dora thought. It was Wilbur's death that had caused her to take comfort in the arms of her teenage neighbor. *Now look what happened*, she thought.

"Reverend Frink is going to raise the roof when he finds out," Dora said to Fannie as the two got on their feet.

"He sho nuff is," Fannie said, "but we just gonna have to cross that bridge when the time comes."

* * *

After Sunday dinner, Reverend Frink and his wife, Louisa, adjourned to the parlor. Reverend Frink read his newspaper while Louisa did her needlepoint. George entered the parlor and stood at the doorway for a while hoping to get his parents' attention. He was nervous. It felt as though butterflies were fluttering around in the pit of his stomach. George cleared his throat. Reverend Frink looked up from his paper.

"Something on your mind son?" he asked.

"Yes, sir," George replied after he cleared his throat again. "Well, sir, um, I need to tell you something."

"Yes, what is it?"

"Dora Smith is pregnant, and I'm the poppa." *There, I got all the words out in one breath*, George thought. Now he braced himself, awaiting his parents' reaction.

Reverend Frink frequently preached to the young people at church about abstinence and against fornication, which was a sin. He preached this same message to his children. However, the message seemed to have escaped his eldest son.

Louisa sat quietly on the sofa anticipating her husband's response. She was mad but didn't want to express her emotions or voice her opinion until after the reverend had spoken.

George stood still as a statue. He knew this news would bring shame on his family and tarnish his father's reputation as a minister. He said nothing for weeks but had known he had to tell them before Romeo and Fannie did.

"Poppa, did you hear me?" George asked. A look passed between Reverend Frink and his wife, which George did not understand.

"I heard you, boy," Reverend Frink responded in a stern voice. "I just can't believe what I'm hearing. How can you bring this shame on your family?" he demanded.

"Poppa, I'm going to do the right thing. I'm going to marry Dora," George replied. "I plan to do right by her and the baby."

His mother tossed her needlepoint onto the sofa. She released an exasperated sigh and folded her arms but did not speak a word.

"Boy, what you talking about?" Reverend Frink said as he stood directly in front of his son, who was slightly taller than his father. "You're already betrothed to the McDonald girl. She's a good Christian girl from a respectable family. What were you doing slipping around with that Dora Smith for anyway?" Reverend Frink ranted. George dropped his head.

"Lord, have mercy, Jesus," Louisa prayed aloud.

Reverend Frink was a strict God-fearing, Bible-thumping minister, who didn't think very highly of his next-door neighbor, Romeo Smith. Romeo worked as the town's wood dealer. He was one of the first black citizens in Southport to own a covered surrey. He used his surrey to make deliveries to the wood sheds of his customers all over town. When he wasn't delivering wood, he used his surrey to taxi people to local destinations around Southport and as far away as Wilmington.

Often referred to as "a man about town," Romeo dressed sharply when taxiing passengers. The six-foot-tall, slender Romeo wore a navy pinstriped, three-piece suit with a red tie and white spats on his black patent leather shoes.

Reverend Frink didn't like the way Romero dressed and referred to him as a prideful peacock. Reverend Frink also didn't like the dark-skinned Dora, who at the age of thirteen had dropped out of school. The now twenty-year-old Dora only had an eighth-grade education and no marketable skill beyond domestic work.

The Frinks wanted much more for their children. More importantly, Reverend Frink didn't believe that Dora was pure.

He once thought he'd seen her coming out of the woodshed with one of the local boys. He had warned George to stay from her, but he obviously hadn't listened.

"Didn't your poppa tell you she was a loose woman?" Louisa interjected, still sitting on the sofa. She feverishly rocked herself back and forth. "Loose women ain't nothing but trouble," she added.

George shifted his eyes though their focus remained on the floor. "I'm sorry," he whispered. "I didn't mean for this to happen. I was just trying to comfort her. She has been having such a hard time ever since her brother Wilbur died. I just—"

"You just what," Reverend Frink interrupted and moved closer to George. They now looked each other in the eyes. "You just wanted to make her feel good?" Reverend Frink snapped. George didn't speak. He simply nodded. "No you just wanted to make yourself feel good. I know the family is grieving over Wilbur. I ain't heartless. But that ain't no excuse for doing what you did with Dora."

"Poppa, I'm sorry," George screamed.

Reverend Frink interjected a scripture from 1 Thessalonians. "'For this is the will of God, even your sanctification that ye should abstain from fornication.' Haven't I taught you the Word of God—what's in the Holy Bible?" Reverend Frink asked.

"Yes, Poppa," George said but quickly responded with Bible passages of his own. "The Bible also said that 'marriage is honorable in all and the bed is undefiled,' and that 'to avoid fornication let every man have his own wife,' and 'it's better to marry than to burn.' So that's why I want to marry Dora."

Reverend Frink glared at George. With squinted eyes, Reverend Frink suddenly slapped George with the back of his right hand. The sudden strike startled his wife, and she involuntarily released a loud gasping sound. She quickly covered her mouth.

"Don't you dare twist the scriptures to suit your own purpose," Reverend Frink said in a low voice. "Let me tell you how it's going to be. You are to have nothing more to do with that woman. I will not allow you to ruin your life like Dora has ruined hers. You will not be marrying Dora. You will marry the McDonald girl as planned. And you are not to acknowledge that child Dora is carrying as yours. Do I make myself clear?"

But it's my child. I have the right to raise it, George screamed inside his head.

He was eighteen years old and about to be married when his seventeen-year-old bride-to-be turned eighteen the following year. Yet he didn't have the courage to stand up to his father on a matter concerning his own future.

Reverend Frink was building a house for George on a plot of land directly behind the Smith's house on Rhett Street. The irony that this child would be living in the house next door to its paternal grandparents and directly behind its father was not lost on George. He sucked in his breath.

"Yes, Poppa, you've made yourself clear."

"Good," Reverend Frink said. "Now, leave my sight," he commanded and pointed toward the doorway.

* * *

Reverend Samuel Frink sat in the parlor during the wee hours of the morning, contemplating the future. He sat slouched down in his wing-backed chair with a blanket draped around his shoulders, his legs crossed at the ankles, and arms, which were folded, rested above his extended stomach. It was as if, in that moment, he was closed to the world outside his door.

Reverend Frink reminisced about his life. The son of former slaves, Samuel Frink had been determined to rise above the stigma of slavery and to become a respectable citizen. What he lacked in formal education, he had made up for in brawn, common sense, and work ethics.

Young Samuel had begun working as a laborer at the age of

sixteen. He had worked as a hod carrier, using a three-sided box called a brick hod to carry bricks and other construction material to support skilled bricklayers. He had thought this work was beneath him because he had secretly believed that having white ancestry had made him more superior than the average black person.

Samuel's father, Parish, was a mulatto, the offspring of a white father and a black mother, making Parish half white. But because Samuel had been the product of a mulatto father and a black mother, he had been considered black with only one-quarter white ancestry at best.

Samuel had met his wife, Louisa, at the St. James Methodist Church in Southport when they were eighteen years old. He had thought she was the most beautiful girl he'd ever seen. Petite, she stood about five foot three inches and had light caramel-colored skin, light brown eyes, and long, curly, brown hair.

She had showed no interest in him, initially, as her mother, Elizabeth, had designs on a well-to-do, white physician named Arthur Dosher for her daughter. Louisa's father had been a white man and had taken care of Elizabeth and Louisa financially until he had died when Louisa was sixteen. Arthur's family had owned the Dosher Plantation. Elizabeth knew that Dr. Dosher had desired Louisa. So she had allowed the twenty-seven-year-old to keep company with her daughter to ensure they both would be taken care of by him. When Elizabeth had told Dr. Dosher the news that Louisa was carrying his child, he had wanted nothing more to do with her.

"I can't have a colored child. It could never inherit my family's estate," he had told Elizabeth. He had ceased providing Louisa and Elizabeth with money and gifts. They had sought solace at the church. Young Samuel had fallen in love with Louisa instantly and had asked the church pastor, Reverend William Breedlove, for guidance about taking up with her. With Elizabeth's permission, Reverend Breedlove had filled Samuel in on Louisa's circumstance.

"She's with child, son," Reverend Breedlove said, "by a white man, who has turned his back on her and the baby. If you married her, you can cover her shame and be a blessing to her and the baby."

The idea of having light-skinned children with a mulatto woman had made Samuel feel superior, and he had agreed to the arranged marriage. Samuel and Louisa had been married within two months. Louisa had given birth to Annie Elizabeth Frink in the fall of 1888. The secret of his wife's shame remained a well-guarded secret.

Since becoming a minister, Reverend Frink had quickly learned that church members expected their preachers to be above reproach. An illegitimate child would ruin his pristine reputation. He would not let anything jeopardize his standing in the church—not even his own unborn grandchild.

Reverend Frink straightened up from his slouching position and stretched his upper body.

"This situation is different than my poor Louisa's unfortunate circumstance," he uttered in a quiet voice. *She was bamboozled by a heinous white man. Dora is a loose woman who is probably trying to trap my boy. Besides, I would hate for George to marry someone so dark skinned.*

Reverend Frink knew Dora's skin tone had little to do with his disapproval of her as a wife for his son. Anyway, he'd learned the hard way that white blood in Negroes didn't count in the world of white people.

"One drop of Negroid genes made you black," a census taker had once told him as he had attempted to explain his mixed lineage. "Well, you look black to me boy, so that's what I'm putting down on this here form," the census taker had said.

No. What Reverend Frink was most concerned about was what his congregation would think or do if word of his son's fornication got out.

Would they condemn me for not practicing what I preached, or worse, would they vote me out as their pastor? He wondered. He was conflicted, but ultimately, it was not a risk he was willing to take.

Young Samuel had worked diligently in the church when his children had just been tykes. Reverend Breedlove had soon elevated him from deacon to assistant pastor. With this position had come a small monthly stipend from the church treasury. When Reverend Breedlove died in 1895, the church had unanimously voted Samuel in as the new pastor of St. James Methodist.

The young Frink family had settled into a house on Nash Street, built by Reverend Frink, who had become, by this time, a skilled carpenter. The home was located less than a mile from the banks of the Cape Fear River. Reverend Frink had taken his ministry seriously and had made sure his family was a shining example of what a good Christian family should be. All his children could recite the books of the Bible, both the Old and New Testaments, and could recite several psalms and prayers.

By 1912, the Frink family had included Annie, who was twenty-four; Eva, who was twenty-one; George, who was eighteen; Grace, who was fifteen; John, who was twelve; Emmett, who was five; and Cora, who was one. With his own family he had proven to the congregation that you could "train up a child in the way he should go, and when he is old he will not depart from it" just as it said in Proverbs 22:6. Reverend Frink would not allow George's mistake to ruin his reputation or to put a cloud of shame over his family.

At dawn, Reverend Frink awoke, still sitting in his parlor chair. He had not realized that he had even fallen asleep. He put his hands to his face and rubbed his eyes. He stretched out his arms in front of him and let out an exasperated groan. His neck was stiff from being in an awkward position. His head throbbed from the situation with George weighing heavily on his mind all night.

He had allowed his anger, hurt, and fear to cloud his judgment. He knew it, but there was no turning back. Everything he had ever preached about forgiveness in his Sunday sermons had not applied in this situation. The circumstances surrounding Annie's conception had been a well-kept secret—even to Annie. This too must remain a secret.

Chapter 26

Just after midnight, on a Friday night in early January of 1913, Dora heard her father, Romeo, stumble into the house. He frequently stayed out late, drinking at the local tavern, first because of Wilbur's death, and now because of Dora's pregnancy. It killed him that his precious Dora would be an unwed mother.

She may as well have a scarlet letter on her forehead, he thought.

He was angry with Dora for bringing shame on the family. After all, she was grown and should have known better. Despite his anger, he felt no malice toward the unborn child. It would be his first grandchild. It was Reverend Frink whom he despised.

"That damn self-righteous son of a bitch Frink," Romeo mumbled. "Who the hell does he think he is?"

Reverend Frink had informed Romeo and Fannie that he would not allow his son to marry their daughter or claim the bastard child she was carrying.

Bastard child, Romeo thought. *He's acting like it ain't his grandchild he's talking about.*

Romeo stood at the sofa and lifted his right leg to remove his boot. He struggled to pull it off. He tugged at the boot and then tugged harder. When he finally got the boot off, he lost his balance and fell backward onto the sofa. Motionless on the sofa,

Romeo clutched the boot to his chest. Tears filled his eyes. He cried himself to sleep shortly thereafter.

Dora tiptoed into the living room as she had done many nights in recent weeks, trying not to disturb her father, who was passed out on the sofa. She gently removed his left boot and then took the right one that he clutched at his chest. Careful not to wake him, she placed the boots on the floor.

As she stood over her sleeping father, Dora looked down and studied his face. She could swear she saw pain etched into every crevice, even as he slept. Watching him, she recalled the conversation between Reverend Frink and her parents the night he came to their house. Dora had listened through the partially opened door of her bedroom.

"Now listen, Mr. Smith. I know you and your family is still grieving over losing your boy. You have my sincere sympathy, truly," Reverend Frink had said. "But George is my oldest son, and he has to set a good example for his younger brothers, John and Emmitt to follow," he continued. "Now, George is promised to marry the McDonald's daughter, Veitha, as soon as she turns eighteen in December."

"Look Rev," Romeo interrupted, "your boy done already told me that he wants to do the right thing by my Dora and that baby. He's eighteen and old enough to make his own decision."

"Well your gal is going on twenty-one and old enough to know better than to spread her legs to a teenager," Reverend Frink had retorted. "Now this is how it's going to be," he continued but had lowered his voice. "George is my son, and I will not allow him to marry your daughter or claim the bastard child she's carrying."

After hearing this, Dora peeked out of her bedroom enough to see the expression on her father's face. Romeo's eyes had narrowed. Dora thought that the look in her father's eyes was so deadly that if they were daggers, Reverend Frink would have surely died from the stab wounds.

Fannie stood beside her husband, from whom she had taken her cue, and had shot daggers at the reverend as well. Sensing the hostility he had created, Reverend Frink abruptly turned on his heels and let himself out of the Smith home.

* * *

Dora released a heavy sigh, covered her father with a blanket, and kissed him softly on the forehead. "Good night, Poppa. I love you," she whispered.

* * *

By mid-February 1913, events, which had occurred in the past few weeks, had taken a physical and emotional toll on Romeo Smith. He sat at the kitchen table drinking a cup of coffee before he went off to work. He thought about his fourteen-year-old son, Wilbur, who had tragically drowned when he had gotten caught in a Cape Fear River current while swimming alone. Now, his girl was pregnant without the benefit of marriage.

Romeo felt like his family was falling apart at the seams. He realized that he was partly to blame for Dora's downfall. She had never had much ambition. Neither he nor his wife had really pushed Dora to do anything with her life.

She will be an unwed mother. I guess that is what she will do with her life, he thought.

Romeo placed his coffee cup in the sink and then put on his winter coat, gloves, and hat and walked toward the back door. Before he could reach for the doorknob, he clutched his chest, gasped, and fell to the floor.

Dora was in her bedroom when she heard a loud thump. *What was that?* She thought she was alone in the house so the noise startled her. She cautiously opened her bedroom door and peeked out. She looked left and right but saw nothing. As she began to walking slowly toward the kitchen entryway, she heard a faint moan in the vicinity of the back door. She walked closer and then saw her father on the floor facedown.

"Poppa," she shrieked, running to him. "Are you all right? What happened?"

Romeo did not answer. Dora pulled at her father's left shoulder, trying to turn him over onto his back. He was heavy, and she exerted great effort to accomplish this. When she finally turned him over, his eyes were closed. She noticed sweat on his brow.

Dora removed his hat, opened his coat, and put her right ear to his chest, trying to hear his heart. She was scared, and it felt like the pit of her stomach was in a knot. She couldn't tell if she was hearing her father's heart beating or her own heart pounding hard and loud in her chest.

Dora pushed her right arm under Romeo's neck and then cradled his head in the bend of her arm. She put her ear close to his lips and felt his shallow breathing on her earlobe.

"Poppa, I'm so sorry. Please forgive me. I never meant to hurt or shame you. Please don't leave me," she whispered.

Romeo opened his eyes. "You're still Poppa's girl," he said in a faint whisper.

"Oh, Poppa," Dora cried. "Hold on. I will go for help."

As Dora was about to stand, Romeo grasped her hand. He looked at her and slowly shook his head. "Don't go," he whispered. A tear dropped from his right eye and rolled down toward his ear. "I don't want to die alone."

"Poppa, I'm just going to run around the corner to get Momma. She will stay with you while I run fetch the doctor."

Romeo mustered all his strength and tightened his gloved grip on Dora's tiny hand. He knew if she left him, even for a few minutes, he would die alone. More tears began to fill his eyes as he looked toward her belly and thought of his unborn grandchild.

"Baby," he whispered.

"What Poppa?" Dora asked.

"Take care of my grandbaby."

In that moment, Dora's heart sank. Her father had never spoken of the baby since he had learned she was pregnant. He had only spoke of the shame that now clouded the Smith name and legacy.

He does love the baby, Dora thought. She began to weep openly and buried her face on her father's chest. After a little while, she raised her head, looked toward him, and gently gave his left shoulder a squeeze.

"I'll take good care of this baby, Poppa. I promise."

Dora had never known her father to be afraid of anything. The physical pain he felt showed on his face, but she could also see fear in his eyes. Romeo's breathing became increasingly labored, and he wheezed like an asthmatic.

Dora began to panic as questions raced through her mind. *What am I going to do? I just can't let him die. I've got to get him some help, but he doesn't want to be alone. Oh God, what should I do?* Dora decided to scream in the hope that someone nearby or passing by would hear.

"Help! Help!" she called. "Poppa, I'm not going to leave the house. I'm just going to see if I can get someone's attention to get help, okay?"

Romeo blinked his eyes once as a sign of agreement. Dora gently removed her right arm, which had been cradling his head. She got up and ran to the kitchen window.

"Help," she screamed. Then she ran to the front door, opened it, and look feverishly up and down the street, hoping to see someone—anyone.

"Somebody help." Dora returned to check on her father. His eyes were closed. Dora fell to her knees beside him and put her ear to his nose. She heard his faint breathing.

"Poppa, can you hear me?" She asked while shaking his left shoulder. She didn't know it, but Romeo had slipped into unconsciousness. Dora's mind began to race. She jumped up and ran out the front door, down the street, and around the corner to the press shop. She hopped up the three steps and flung open the door, causing the bell at the top to jangle in alarm.

"Momma," she called out. Fannie came running from the back.

"Chil', what in tarnation are you doing out here without your coat in the middle of winter? You gonna catch your death."

"Momma, its Poppa. He fell out on the floor in the kitchen. Go home to him now. I'm going to get the doctor."

"Oh, my God, chil', what happen?" Fannie asked in a panic.

"I don't know. Just go," Dora commanded, exiting the shop. Dora ran the five blocks to the doctor's office. When she arrived, she flung open the door and practically fell in. The nurse sitting at the desk jumped to her feet when Dora entered.

"Are you all right?" She asked running over to the pregnant young woman. Dora tried to catch her breath and speak at the same time.

"We need Dr. Treadway. It's my father. He's barely breathing."

"I'm sorry," said the nurse with an empathetic expression on her face. "The doctor is out on another call."

"Oh no, no, no," Dora screamed, falling to her knees. "My poppa needs help now," she shrieked.

"Okay," the nurse said, trying to calm Dora down. "I'll go back with you and take a look at him. Just give me a minute."

The nurse ran to the back of the office and grabbed the extra medical bag. She took a blanket from the supply room. She then retrieved her coat from the closet and headed back to the waiting area where Dora remained on her knees, crying and covering her face with her hands.

"Come on now," the nurse said to Dora as she wrapped the blanket around her. "I'm going to lock up here, and you can take me to your father. What's your name and address? I'm going to leave a note for the doctor when he returns."

After Dora gave the nurse her information, she quickly led the nurse to her house. The blanket wrapped around Dora flapped backward in the cold winter's wind.

Please don't let it be too late, she prayed.

Dora burst through the front door and ran straight to the kitchen with the nurse following her.

"Momma, I'm back," she called out. "The doctor was out, but I brought the nurse."

Fannie was kneeling at her husband's side. She had placed a bed pillow under his head and a cool cloth on his forehead. She was motionless with a glazed look in her eyes. Her face was tear-stained.

"Ma'am," the nurse said, "I'm Hazel, Dr. Treadway's nurse. I'm going to examine your husband. Is that all right?"

Fannie nodded. Hazel knelt down across from Fannie. She removed the stethoscope from the medical bag and placed the earpieces in her ears. She unbuttoned Romeo's shirt, placed the head of the instrument on his chest, and listened for a heartbeat. Dora stood anxiously behind the nurse shivering with the blanket from the doctor's office wrapped tightly around her. Hazel moved the stethoscope a little to the left and then to the right, but she couldn't hear a heartbeat. She placed her fingers on his neck for a moment but couldn't feel a pulse. She shut her eyes tightly and then released a heavy sigh.

"I'm sorry," she said, "he's gone."

Fannie threw herself onto Romeo's chest and sobbed. "Why, God, why?" she cried.

Nurse Hazel stood and faced Dora. "Is there anyone I should contact for you?" she asked.

Dora lowered her head. "Just my little sister, Alethia," she replied in a soft voice. "She's in school. We should bring her home now and tell her about Poppa."

Just then, a knock came at the front door. "Hello," a voice called out. It was the doctor entering the already opened door.

"Come in," Nurse Hazel called while walking toward the front of the house. "Doctor, I'm afraid the patient has expired—a possible heart attack," she said in a subdued tone of voice. "The wife and daughter are in the kitchen with the body. I'm going to walk down to the school and bring the younger daughter home."

"Thanks, Hazel," said the doctor. "I'll make arrangements for the funeral director to pick up the body."

On February 20, 1913, the funeral service for Romeo Smith was held at Mount Zion Baptist Church—the same church where his son Wilbur's memorial service had been held five months earlier. Romeo was dressed in his three-piece, navy, striped suit and red tie—the attire he was famous for wearing when taxiing passengers in his surrey. Fannie wore a black dress with pearl ear clips. A black laced veil covered her face. Dora and Alethia wore matching black dresses with white-laced collars.

The organist played "Nearer My God to Thee." The minister spoke about Romeo's life and the loved ones he had left behind. He tried to comfort the family by saying that both Romeo and Wilbur were together now in heaven. However, Fannie felt little comfort. Her husband of more than twenty years was never coming home again.

As the funeral procession filed from the church and followed the pine wood casket that held Romeo's body, Fannie watched Romeo's friends carefully carry his coffin out of the church. She felt as if a cauldron was bubbling up and overflowing from deep within her soul.

When she reached the back of the sanctuary, she saw George and his father, Reverend Frink, standing at the last pew. As Fannie was about to pass them, Reverend Frink stepped out into the aisle, reached out, and touched her forearm. She stopped in her tracks. Every muscle in her body stiffened. Her eyes, bloodshot and red from crying, were fixed on his hand on her arm. She thought she felt her skin crawl.

"Mrs. Smith, I am so sorry for your loss," Reverend Frink

offered in a way of a condolence. George stood behind his father in silence. His face revealed signs of having cried hard. He had longed to be with Dora and her family to provide support, but his father had forbidden it.

Fannie's eyes darted back and forth from Reverend Frink's eyes to his hand on her arm. She sucked in her breath and contorted her lips. She remembered the last time that Reverend Frink had been in her house, and how his only concern had been for his son's future and his family's reputation.

He didn't seem to give a damn about our family's reputation. Always looking down on us like we're just a house full of sinners, Fannie thought. She looked at Reverend Frink with a stoic expression and said in a quiet but stern voice, "You go to hell, sir."

Chapter 27

On May 31, 1913, George Frink married Veitha McDonald. Reverend Frink asked the seventeen-year-old Veitha's parents' permission to move up the wedding from the previously planned December date. The reason for the request was that his wife, Louisa, was now two months pregnant with their eighth child, which was due in December. However, Reverend Frink's real motive for the spring wedding was an attempt to get George's mind off Dora's baby, which was due in August.

Things were going according to Reverend Frink's plans. His standing as a minister and his family's good name and reputation remained intact. However, as the lives of the Frink family seemed to flourish, Fannie and her daughters' lives seemed to diminish.

After Romeo's death, they struggled financially. The money Romeo had earned from wood dealing and taxiing was sorely missed. Fannie asked Romeo's brother, John from Wilmington to help them sell his surrey for a good price. But money was still tight when Fannie became the sole wage earner.

By July, Dora was in the eighth month of her pregnancy. She had worked at the press shop with her mother through the end of June. She had to stop because the work had become too hard on her—especially on her feet and lower back.

One Saturday morning, Dora awoke and remembered that it

would have been Wilbur's fifteenth birthday that day. She rocked gently in her bed from side to side until she was able to swing her feet out of bed and place them on the floor. She walked gingerly, placing one foot in front of the other and grimacing at the pain her weight put on her feet until she reached the kitchen where Fannie and Alethia were having breakfast.

"Well, good morning, sleepyhead," said Fannie.

"Morning, Doe," Alethia said with a mouthful of oatmeal.

"Good morning," Dora replied. "Today would have been Wilbur's fifteenth birthday. I was thinking we could remember him today by making a chocolate cake—his favorite."

Fannie sat at the kitchen table sipping her coffee and smiled. "I think that's a fine idea," she said quietly as fond memories of her son crossed her mind. She recalled when he turned thirteen how tall he seemed to sprout up overnight. He was going to be at least six feet tall just like his poppa. She was sure of that.

Alethia chimed in, "Yeah, that's a good idea. Do we have all the ingredients?"

"Probably not enough of everything," Dora replied, "but we can go down to market later to get everything we need."

Around noon, Dora, Fannie, and Alethia entered the local grocers. Fannie and Alethia began collecting the items needed for the cake while a tired Dora stood near the entrance of the store fanning herself with her wide straw hat. Two women gave her disapproving glares as they passed her to leave the store.

What's their problem? Dora thought. She looked at the women with narrowed eyes and contorted lips. *They acting like they never seen an unwed pregnant woman.*

Just then, Louisa Frink and her daughter, Annie, entered the store. Dora's eyes widened when she saw Louisa's extended round belly.

What the … she's pregnant too? She thought.

Fannie had paid for her grocery items, and she and Alethia were walking toward Dora just as the Frink women came in the store. Everyone paused at the entryway not saying a word.

Louisa gazed at Dora's belly for several seconds and then cut her eyes over and stared at Fannie. She remembered when her husband had gathered the older family members together to tell them about George's sin of fornication. Rather than let the townspeople and, more importantly, the church members know of George's shameful actions, Reverend Frink had forbidden them to accept or to acknowledge the child.

Louisa started to open her mouth to speak but stopped herself. The decision had been made and there was nothing more to say. Louisa's trancelike state was broken when her daughter, Annie, grabbed Louisa under the arm and pulled her away.

"Come on Momma," she said. The two women entered the store.

Fannie watched as they walked away. *Stuck up mulatto bitches,* she thought. "Come on, girls. Let's go home," she said.

* * *

Early Sunday morning on August 31, 1913, the Frink family sat down for breakfast that daughters Annie and Eva had prepared. As Annie put a plate in front of her mother, she leaned down and kissed her on the cheek. "Good morning, Momma. Happy birthday."

"Thank you, baby," Louisa said. All the children approached their mother with a kiss and a birthday greeting. They all sat at the table and waited for their father.

"Good morning, everyone," Reverend Frink said as he entered the dining room. He leaned over and kissed his wife. "Happy birthday, my dear," he whispered in her ear.

"Thank you, sweetheart," she responded with a sheepish smile. Although her marriage had been arranged, Louisa had grown to love and to respect her husband.

Eva placed a plate in front of her father, and they all bowed their heads for the blessing of the food. After breakfast, Reverend Frink, George, his wife Veitha, Grace, John, and Emmett prepared to leave for church services. Annie and Eva stayed home with their mother and little Cora. At the age of forty-four and now six months pregnant, the doctor had cautioned Louisa to take it easy for the duration of her pregnancy.

Once outside, George saw Alethia Smith running frantically down the street.

"Whoa. Slow down," George said stepping into her path to stop her. "What's going on?"

"It's Doe. I have to get the doctor," she said as she broke free of George's hold and continued running down the street.

George looked in the direction of the Smith house. Knowing what George was thinking, Reverend Frink said, "Come on, boy. Let's go. There ain't nothing you can do."

George's mind was on Dora and the birth of his child during the entire three-hour church service. After the benediction, he ran out of the church, without a word to anyone, and raced to see about Dora. He feverishly knocked at the door and was met by Alethia.

"What do you want?" she asked in an abrupt manner.

"Has the baby come yet?"

"No, Doe is still in labor. It's taking forever. The doctor and Momma are in the bedroom with her. You can wait here in the kitchen with me if you want.

Sitting at the kitchen table and sipping iced tea, Alethia and George could hear Dora's screams becoming more prevalent.

"Okay, Dora, now push," Dr. Treadway said.

"Ugh. I can't. It hurts," Dora screamed in agony.

"It's supposed to hurt, chil'," Fannie yelled, bracing Dora's back. "Come on. Womenfolk been birthing babies since the beginning of time. You can do it too. Now push," Fannie screamed.

Dora propped herself up on her elbows and held tightly to the bed sheets. She used the footboard of the bed to brace her feet and pushed with all her strength.

"Good girl," Dr. Treadway said. "I see the baby's head." After several more pushes, the baby was finally out.

"Congratulations! It's a boy," said Dr. Treadway.

"Thank you, Jesus," said Fannie, wiping the sweat from her brow.

"Yes, thank you, Jesus," Dora said exhausted as she flopped back down on the bed.

After cleaning the baby, Fannie looked down proudly at the newborn in her arms. With tears in her eyes, she remembered her husband and her son. She walked over to Dora's bedside and placed the baby in her daughter's arms.

"He's beautiful," Fannie said, bending down to kiss Dora's forehead.

Fannie exited the room and walked into the kitchen where George and Alethia still sat at the kitchen table. When Fannie approached, they both leapt to their feet. They had heard the baby cry and looked expectedly at Fannie.

"You two can go in," Fannie told Alethia and George. "We got ourselves a healthy boy."

George felt his heart leap with joy. *A boy*, he thought. *I have a son.*

After hearing the news, George and Alethia headed toward Dora's room, both trying to enter through the doorway at the same time.

"Sorry, you go first," George said.

As Alethia approached the bed where Dora and the baby lay, Dora moved back the blanket so that her sister and George could get a good look.

"Doe, he's beautiful," Alethia said, looking down at the baby in her sister's arms. "What will you name him?"

"I was thinking about naming him Romeo after Poppa or

maybe Wilbur." Dora looked over at her mother, who was back in the bedroom, for approval.

"Aw, that's sweet of you, chil', but I don't think I could bare that," she said, wiping a tear from her eye and appreciating the thoughtful gesture

"What about naming him John Brown Smith after John Brown," Alethia interjected.

"Who?" Dora asked.

"John Brown, the abolitionist," Alethia answered.

"Oh," Dora said pretending to know what an abolitionist was. "Well, I like the name John, but I'd rather name him after Uncle John. And I don't like Brown for the middle name."

"What about Frederick for the middle name?" George chimed in.

"So, who's Frederick?" Alethia asked.

"Have you heard of Frederick Douglass?"

"Yes," Alethia exclaimed. He was an abolitionist too.

"That's right," George replied.

"I like that," Alethia said.

"Sounds good to me," said Dora. "Momma, what do you think about us naming this little guy John Frederick Smith?"

Fannie smiled. "That sounds like a fine name, chil'.

George grimaced when he heard Smith at the end of the name. He was pleased to have had a small part in naming his son, but it was bittersweet. He recalled a conversation with his father regarding what he called "George's little illegitimate." If it was a boy, George really wanted to name the baby George Franklin Frink Junior, but his father had forbidden it.

"That child will not sully the Frink name," his father had said. "In fact, I better not hear that the baby has any part or any version of your name."

"Great, we'll call him Freddie," said Alethia, interrupting George's thoughts. "How do you like your name, little Freddie?"

she asked the infant while stroking the fuzzy brown hair on the top of his head.

* * *

It was after dark when George finally left the Smith home. Before returning to his own house, he went next door to his parents' house. When he entered, he found his parents sitting in the parlor. Reverend Frink was reading a passage from the Bible to his wife. He was still wearing his church attire, which was a plain brown three-piece suit. Louisa was in her robe. George paused at the entryway of the parlor. Without making eye contact with them, he announced in a low voice, "It's a boy."

Chapter 28

OXON HILL, MARYLAND

March 19, 1983

Fred lay in bed gazing at the ceiling with his eyes fixed on the light fixture. He continued to stare as the light appeared to miraculously change into the form of an angel. He closed his eyes, but he could still see the angelic form as visual mental imagery.

"Fred, are you asleep?" Elsie asked from the other bed in the room. He had been released from Malcolm Grow Medical Center on Andrews Air Force Base just days earlier. He was at the end stages of emphysema. A smoker for nearly forty years, Fred had been diagnosed with the disease in 1979, when he was sixty-six years old.

He would spend the next three and a half years in and out of the hospital. His most recent stay at Malcolm Grow lasted twenty-one days. It had been a most contentious time for both Elsie and the hospital staff. Fred often complained when his wife didn't come to visit every day, stay longer, or get him released sooner. For the nursing staff, Fred gave a right hook for anyone who came near him with a hypodermic needle, thermometer, or blood pressure cuff.

During one visit, Elsie arrived to find Fred in a deep sleep.

After an hour had passed and he had not awakened, she became concerned. She walked down the hall to the nurse's station to inquire about her husband's condition.

"Excuse me. Why is Sergeant Smith sleeping so long? I've been here for over an hour," Elsie asked the two nurses sitting behind the desk.

"I had to give him a strong sedative," one nurse replied.

"Why?" Elsie asked. Having been a nurse herself for many years, Elsie could not fathom why this nurse thought it necessary to give him such a strong dosage.

"Because," the nurse replied with a smirk on her face, "if I didn't knock him out, he was going to knock me out."

"What?" Elsie questioned.

"Yes," the nurse continued, "Sergeant Smith has been punching different nurses all week."

"Punching them?" Elsie's voice cracked.

"Yes ma'am. He hit Nurse Evelyn here, square in the mouth, the other day, and her lip was swollen." The one nurse pointed at her colleague who affirmed the testimony with a slight nod.

Elsie released an exasperated sigh like air escaping from a balloon. "Oh my God, I can't believe this," she said.

Outwardly, Elsie expressed disbelief at her husband's action, but deep down, she knew Fred could be nasty, at times, and was quite capable of this behavior. Once when they had argued, she had referred to his mother as "Mammy." This term was especially offensive in the southern black culture, and Fred found it highly insulting. In quick response, Fred had swung at Elsie's face and had barely clipped her chin with an open hand. Equally quick to react, Elsie had grabbed a table lamp and clobbered Fred on the head. The light bulb exploded and sounded like a gunshot.

She also recalled a time Fred had become perturbed with her for not bringing him the right meal replacement shake. After bringing Fred two different flavors at two different times, he still wasn't satisfied.

"Psst," Fred had said, trying to get Elsie's attention.

She had hated that sound. She had cringed before responding. "What is it now, Fred?"

"How about you bring me an eggnog flavored shake?" Fred asked in a voice just above a whisper.

"No," Elsie said, "I'm not going to get it." She continued to sit on her bed reading her book.

After a long pause, Fred had, once again, tried to get her attention. "Psst, are you going to get me that eggnog shake?" Fred had asked.

"I brought you a vanilla shake. You took two sips and sent it back," Elsie said in a stern tone. "Then you wanted a chocolate shake so I brought that, and you said you didn't want it. So, no, I'm not going a third time to get you a shake you'll just refuse and have me trotting back to the kitchen for." Fred had balled his frail, withered fist and symbolically spat on it.

"What would you do if I put these five across your lips?" Fred had asked, leaning forward and looking her square in the eyes. The piercing look in Fred's brown eyes had been enough to let Elsie know that he was serious.

So with equally steel-piercing eyes she responded, "If you put those five across my lips, I'm going to slap the cat-walking shit out of you." Her voice had been low and deadly. She had never broken her gaze.

Fred's expression quickly changed. His eyes widened. He retracted his head. After a long pause, he had begun to chuckle.

"I believe you would," he said. Elsie's medical training had made her all too aware that many times, people with terminal illnesses turned on their caregivers.

"So today when I went to his room to take his vitals," the nurse continued, interrupting Elsie's thoughts, "he said he was going to knock me out. That's when I decided to give him the sedative. I figured I would knock him out before he knocked me out." Elsie could do nothing but shake her head.

The following day when Elsie visited Fred, he was sitting up in his bed, alert and determined to leave the hospital. He had devised a plan of escape and was anxious to share his plan with her.

"Elsie," he said as she entered his hospital room, "I'm getting out of here tonight. Here's what I want you to do. You get our little daughter to wait on the beach in the car with the motor running. Then get them two strong strapping sons of ours to come and get on each side and carry me out of here while you distract the doctor."

Elsie realized that, in his mind at that moment, Fred thought he was back on Elgin Air Force Base in Fort Walton Beach, Florida. She knew she had to get him out of the hospital and back into the comforts of his own home. His condition was terminal, and his days were few. He knew it too. The sterile environment of the drab military hospital was not how Elsie wanted Fred to spend his final days.

"No, Fred," she said patting him on the shoulder. "We don't have to break you out of here like a criminal. Let me talk to the doctor."

Fred leaned back on his pillow. With the help of the oxygen tank, he breathed a sigh of relief. Elsie exited the room and walked toward the nurse's station. On the way, she spotted one of Fred's doctors coming down the hall and stopped him.

"Doctor, may I talk to you?" She asked as she approached him.

"Of course," said the doctor.

"Listen. You and I both know that Sergeant Smith is dying, and he knows it too. He wants to go home to die. What can you do to make that happen? I'm a nurse, and I can take care of him at home with the proper equipment."

"Okay, Mrs. Smith," the doctor replied. "I can make arrangements today for you to borrow a hospital bed, portable commode, and oxygen tanks. Once the equipment is delivered and set up in your home, we will transport him back home by ambulance."

"Thank you, doctor. How soon can we have him back home?"

"He should be home sometime on Friday."

* * *

Fred opened his eyes and stared back up at the ceiling light.

"Freddie, are you asleep?" He heard his wife ask. He looked over in her direction.

"I'm awake," he answered in a hoarse voice.

"Good, because it's almost time for your favorite show with the little bad boy," Elsie said. She was referring to the situation comedy *Diff'rent Strokes*. Fred always got a kick out of Gary Coleman's character Arnold's catch phrase, "What you talking about Willis?"

She got up and cranked the head of his bed up so he could view the program. They watched the thirty-minute episode, which guest starred First Lady Nancy Reagan. After the show, Elsie helped Fred get onto the portable commode.

"Give me a little wipe," Fred said when he was finished. Elsie pulled some toilet paper from the roll and steadied him.

With smiling eyes, Elsie answered, "Wipe yourself."

Fred smirked, taking the toilet paper. After he was finished, he leaned his five-foot, eleven-inch, frail frame on his wife's five-foot, three-inch body as she led him back to his bed. She returned to her bed and continued reading her book.

After several minutes, Elsie suddenly felt a profound stillness in the room. Although the television was still on, she couldn't shake the feeling that something in the room had changed. She looked over at Fred, who was staring at the ceiling light. She heard a strange sound coming from his direction so she lowered the volume on the television. Then she realized that the strange sound she heard was the unmistakable death rattle. As a trained nurse, Elsie recognized the gurgling sound a person makes during the dying process. This happens when a person is no longer able to swallow or cough.

"Huh?" Elsie heard Fred whisper. She slightly craned her neck forward and cocked her ear. "I'm coming, Momma," Fred whispered again.

Elsie now focused on the sound of the oxygen tank. She realized that at some point Fred had taken the oxygen tube out of his nose.

"Fred," she called out, but got no answer. She rose from her bed and walked over to him. She leaned down and put her face within inches of his.

"Liz," Elsie called out to her daughter, who was in the living room. "I think Daddy is dead." When Liz arrived at the door of her parents' bedroom, she saw her mother checking her father's pulse.

"Yes, he's dead," Elsie confirmed. In shock, Liz did an immediate about face and exited the room.

* * *

March 24, 1983

Liz sat stoically in the back seat of the funeral car on the return drive home from her father's interment. She continued to wear her metaphoric mask of bravery. She held this outward appearance because it was her family's way. The Smith family did not express emotion, and they certainly did not expose the cracks in their foundation. So they appeared unmoved by the grief and indifferent to the pain. No one was better at this façade than Liz.

She reminded herself that she had been a good daughter to her father—dare she say even a perfect daughter. She had done nothing to shame her father or her family. She had been his pride and joy. But the pedestal he'd placed her on had sometimes been too high for her and had put her under a great deal of pressure.

She had feared she would eventually disappoint him, but she

never did. However, the cost of being the good and dutiful daughter had come with a price. Liz felt that she'd missed out on having a real childhood, and she resented it. She resented always being the sensible and responsible one in the family. The weight of this burden would not be lightened with her father's death, because her mother, who needed her now more than ever, would still expect to see a *perfect* Liz.

When the gold funeral car finally pulled up to the apartment building, Liz was the first to leap out. She didn't look back and was relieved that she would never have to see that ugly colored vehicle again. She hopped up the three steps of the building, anxious to get out of the bitter cold. She flung open the door to the apartment and walked through the threshold.

When she entered the room, she immediately saw Fred's apricot swivel chair. It was empty. Liz felt a dull ache in her chest. She had a sense of something squeezing her heart. A blockage seemed to form in her throat. She swallowed hard. As the family all gathered in the living room of the garden apartment, the urge to escape overwhelmed Liz.

I've got to get out of here, she thought.

She made a beeline to her bedroom and closed the door. This was her sanctuary—the place where she could be alone with her feelings. She threw herself on the bed and began to cry. The tears flowed like a broken dam. When she thought her cries would become loud enough to penetrate the four walls of her bedroom, she buried her face in her pillow. She didn't want anyone to come in to see about her. She didn't want to be comforted. The hurt, the disappointment, and the shame were all she had left of her father.

After a while, Liz became exhausted, both mentally and physically. She remembered her mother's story about Fred calling out to his mother before he had died. Her brothers also shared with her a phenomenon they had witnessed where a vapor-like substance floated upward toward the heavens right after Fred had died. Both brothers had been standing on the patio when they had seen the *miracle*. Liz was disappointed that she had missed out on the spiritual events that her mother and brothers had experienced concerning Fred.

As Liz lay on her bed squeezing her pillow, she drifted off to sleep. She began dreaming of her father's ascent to the other side.